Paragraph

A Journal of Modern Critical Theory

Volume 35, Number 1, March 2012

Bourdieu and the Literary Field

Edited by Jeremy Ahearne and John Speller

Contents

Introduction: Bourdieu and the Literary Field
JEREMY AHEARNE AND JOHN SPELLER 1

How Field Theory Can Contribute to Knowledge of World
Literary Space
ANNA BOSCHETTI 10

Autonomy Revisited: The Question of Mediations and its
Methodological Implications
GISÈLE SAPIRO 30

The Literary Field and the Field of Power: The Case of Modern
China
MICHEL HOCKX 49

Between Repression and Anamnesis: Pierre Bourdieu and the
Vicissitudes of Literary Form
JEREMY F. LANE 66

Reading and Reflexivity: Bourdieu's Faulkner
JOHN SPELLER 83

Fields and Fragments: Bourdieu, Pascal and the Teachings
of Literature
JEREMY AHEARNE 97

T0371008

On an Enigmatic Text by Pierre Bourdieu
JÉRÔME DAVID   115

Apollinaire, Autumn Ill
PIERRE BOURDIEU   131

Notes on Contributors   137

Paragraph is indexed in the Arts & Humanities Citation Index and
Current Contents/Arts & Humanities

Introduction: Bourdieu and the Literary Field

JEREMY AHEARNE AND JOHN SPELLER

Pierre Bourdieu's range as a thinker was extremely wide, and it would be misleading to present him primarily as a literary theorist. Trained as a philosopher, he became the leading French sociologist of his generation, and brought under the spotlight of his 'critical sociology' a whole series of institutional and discursive universes (education, art, linguistics, public administration, politics, philosophy, journalism, economics and others).[1] Far from representing an intellectual dispersal, these manifold objects of enquiry allowed him to develop and refine a comprehensive theory of social process and power-relations based on distinctive concepts such as 'field', 'habitus', variously conceived notions of 'capital', and '*illusio*' (all these concepts and others will be explicated and assessed in this issue). Yet Bourdieu's analyses were scarcely ever received as neutral descriptions within the fields which he analysed. Bourdieu's abiding agenda was to show how the discursive presuppositions and institutional logics at work in such fields carried but also masked certain social logics that a 'critical sociology' could disclose. Coupled with the inveterately combative drive seldom absent from Bourdieu's objectifying analyses — and even setting aside the misprisions to which an external analyst is inevitably subject — this helps explain the resistance which his work recurrently provoked.[2] In this respect, Bourdieu's forays into the world of literary studies and his reception therein can be seen as part of a wider pattern.

When it appeared in 1992, *The Rules of Art* was perceived by many to represent, at worst, an all-out attack on approaches to literature in the academy, or, at best, a comprehensive endeavour to annex literary study under an all-embracing sociology.[3] To some degree, this resistance simply reactivated an older hostility among literary scholars to the 'reductionism' of sociology. This was unfortunate,

Paragraph 35.1 (2012): 1–9
DOI: 10.3366/para.2012.0038
© Edinburgh University Press
www.eupjournals.com/para

insofar as Bourdieu's theory of literary autonomy takes shape precisely in reaction to such traditional sociological reductionism. The concern about annexation does respond to a certain scientific imperialism that often emanates from Bourdieu's writing, and this will be addressed by a number of contributors to the present special issue. At the same time, however, the refusal to engage with Bourdieu's work on these grounds is also unfortunate. As several contributors also show, the coordinated analysis of literary worlds — including the worlds of literary form — as relationally constructed social 'fields', with their diverse forms of 'habitus', 'capital' and '*illusio*', can generate significant insight into those worlds. Finally, there are also, paradoxically perhaps, dangers in reducing Bourdieu's own thinking on (and with) literature to his explicit 'theory' of literature, as expressed most systematically in *The Rules of Art*. Literature is sometimes his object; but, as some of the articles included in this issue will show, he is also at times, to a degree unusual among sociologists, its subject.

Literature was in fact of long-standing interest to Pierre Bourdieu, personally, theoretically and politically. As a boy, he imagined being another Balzac.[4] He published intermittently on literature throughout his academic career, from his 1966 article 'Champ intellectuel et projet créateur' ('Intellectual Field and Creative Project') to what was, as it happens, his last piece of major empirical research, 'Une révolution conservatrice dans l'édition' ('A Conservative Revolution in Publishing') (1999).[5] References to literature appear recurrently across an œuvre that that comprises several hundred articles and some thirty books. His major work on literature was his 1992 book *The Rules of Art*, but this was a synthesis of ideas and articles written and developed over the previous decades. Bourdieu spent much of his time not simply 'attacking' literature, as a common misrepresentation sometimes suggests, but vigorously defending both it and the cultural ecosystem on which it depends. Towards the end of his career, when he took a more stridently political turn, the sociologist warned with what can seem like striking prescience of the threats to intellectual autonomy posed by the withdrawal of State support for the arts, the submission of education to the needs of the economy and the erosion of what he called the 'social conditions of existence' of humanistic culture, including publishing houses, journals and bookshops. Moreover, Bourdieu's ongoing engagement with literature was not limited simply to the insight it can or cannot provide into social reality. In 1995, in an article translated for the first time in the present issue, we see him turning to a poem by Guillaume Apollinaire (as he would turn in 1998 to Blaise Pascal) to meditate on illness, death and his autumn years.[6]

The interest of a special issue on Pierre Bourdieu and the literary field is at least twofold. On the one hand, it will shed light on an important but often under-examined component in Bourdieu's intellectual project, with significant ramifications for our understanding of his entire œuvre. On the other hand, Bourdieu's work offers literary researchers a comprehensively articulated theory and method, together with a corpus of empirical case studies on which to build. The collected contributions to the issue variously combine these two interrelated centres of interest, moving from more programmatic overviews of Bourdieu's theoretical apparatus and its applications to detailed studies of what Bourdieu effectively 'does' with selected literary writers. Articles by Gisèle Sapiro and Anna Boschetti set out the broad theoretical framework Bourdieu applies to literature, and demonstrate how it has been collectively taken up by other researchers, focusing respectively on the themes of mediation and autonomy and on fields and world literary space. Michel Hockx shows how this theoretical framework can be and has been applied to the particular case of literary writing in China (this was not a possibility that Bourdieu had imagined). Articles by Jeremy Lane, John Speller and Jeremy Ahearne then examine different aspects of Bourdieu's own work on literature 'in practice', and find important points both of continuity and divergence with regard to his theoretical prescriptions and wider work. Their articles focus on Bourdieu's work on Flaubert in relation to notions of repression and anamnesis; on an overlooked article on Faulkner that illuminates his theories of reading and reflexivity; and on his attitude towards and use of literature through an exploration of his transepochal 'collaboration' with Blaise Pascal. Jérôme David seeks, finally, to elucidate the singularity of an enigmatic text, mentioned already, by Bourdieu on Apollinaire, in which his reflections on the poem, death and dying challenge us to modify our understanding of Bourdieu's own affective disposition (his 'habitus'), and of literature's place within it. The editors are grateful to Bourdieu's estate and to *Cahiers d'Histoire des littératures romanes/Romanistische Zeitschrift für Literaturgeschichte* for permission to translate and publish, as an appendix to this issue, the Bourdieu article in question, 'Apollinaire, Automne malade', for the first time in English.

In the first article in this collection, Anna Boschetti provides a general overview of Bourdieu's method, setting out the principles of Bourdieu's overall sociologocial/anthropological theory (as developed in *The Craft of Sociology* (1968) and beyond), while helpfully relating this theory in broad terms to its anglophone foil (individualism and interactionism). The author probes certain perceived weak spots of Bourdieu's extant studies of literature (the naturalization of the concept of the 'field'; the privileging of already canonized literary figures; their restriction to the national level), insofar as these impede the full development of his theories' potential. Boschetti also explores the ways in which aspects of his theories have been unfolded and adapted by researchers working on literature, in particular how field theory can be used in the relational study of literatures across national and transnational spaces. Indeed, one of the most important points Boschetti makes is that the analysis of specific cases, which are by definition limited and circumscribed, can be reconciled with a worldwide perspective, by producing comparable studies making use of common principles and standards. Boschetti draws on a broad range of secondary sources to present Bourdieu's theory of literature as it is caught up today in an elaborate and sophisticated collective work of adaptation and refinement. Rather than a closed system of concepts, Boschetti argues that Bourdieu's theory is a continual work in progress, which continues to be developed through collective effort involving its use in different empirical contexts and the comparison of results.

In the second article, Gisèle Sapiro takes questions of 'mediation' as a practical focus in exploring the development of a Bourdieusian-based approach to analyses of literary works and fields. The 'mediation' in question revolves essentially around the relation between 'internal' and 'external' approaches to the analysis of literary production and reception, and the relations between 'autonomous' and 'heteronomous' principles underlying the creation and judgement of literary works. The notions of autonomy and mediation are important both for a fundamental understanding of Bourdieu's theory and for an appreciation of the normative cultural and political implications that he and other researchers draw out of it. Sapiro explores three broad levels at which the interplay between internal and external perspectives and between autonomous and heteronomous modes of determination can be studied. These treat, respectively, the external material and ideological conditions for the production of works, the space of position-takings and stylistic possibilities as they appear to differently situated agents within literary or artistic fields, and questions of reception (essentially in terms of critical reception). Sapiro does not simply oppose 'internal' and 'external' analysis, but shows instead how these two broad approaches can be interwoven. Likewise, she does not pit principles of autonomy and heteronomy against each other in monolithic fashion, but rather shows how the writings of Bourdieu and other researchers allow us to draw out forms of complex and sometimes paradoxical dialectic at work.

Michel Hockx focuses on the interest scholars of Chinese literature, both anglophone and sinophone, have found in Pierre Bourdieu's sociological theory of literature. The underlying argument is that Bourdieu's mode of construing the relative autonomy of the literary field has provided analysts of Chinese literature with a means of moving beyond the flattening effects of one-dimensionally politicized approaches (even if these latter have taken the opposing forms of support for and hostility to a political regime, whether from commentators based inside or outside China). Certainly, the interest of Bourdieu's work heretofore has tended to be in its capacity to integrate various 'contexts' rather than its analysis of intrinsic form. Nonetheless, the article does show also how certain types of literary form (notably in the 1980s) can be seen as having played out in unexpected ways when effective contexts are suitably illuminated. The article thus introduces not only a rich vein of research into Chinese literature, but also demonstrates the potential of Bourdieu's theories to be applied to very different national traditions, also seen in the macro-context of World Literary Space. Overall, Hockx's article is particularly interesting insofar as it shows the uses of Bourdieu's paradigm, often rather glibly accused of being 'francocentric', when transposed, applied and tested in a very different context.

Jeremy Lane writes to some extent against a certain current of thought that relativizes the value of Bourdieu's work on literature by saying that it has little to say on literary form as such (thus in effect amalgamating Bourdieu's work with a certain 'externalizing' tendency in the sociology of literature). The author stresses by contrast Bourdieu's recurrent focus on the functions of form as such, particularly in relation to his work on Flaubert. The author goes on to draw out two broad functions of form that are developed by Bourdieu in largely compartmentalized manner. On the one hand, form can 'euphemize' or veil the reality it purports to represent. On the other hand, via various forms of aesthetic shock or defamiliarization, it can bring that reality into fuller consciousness (*anamnesis*). The author also discusses two modes of understanding the 'disclosing' that form can operate — on the one hand in analogy with dreamwork and its interpretation; on the other hand as the rendering explicit as such of socio-cognitive-affective structures that operate implicitly through the habitus. Indeed Lane perceives basic conflicts both between the two accounts Bourdieu gives of the functions of Flaubert's literary form, and between the two models for understanding the disclosure of what the agent has 'repressed' or 'forgotten'. The author suggests that these vicissitudes and contradictions in Bourdieu's accounts of literary form might themselves be interpreted as a return of a repressed truth: that of sociology's inheritance from and debt to literature and literary writers such as Victor Hugo and Honoré de Balzac, who were the first to realize sociology's ambition to offer a comprehensive account of society and culture.

In 'Reading and Reflexivity: Bourdieu's Faulkner', John Speller examines a previously overlooked essay by Bourdieu on the author from Mississippi, tucked away in the final pages of *The Rules of Art*. After five hundred pages extolling contextualizing field analysis, we come to a purely internal reading of William Faulker's short story 'A Rose for Emily'. Speller tries to unravel this puzzle left at the end of *The Rules*, a task that takes him into a discussion of Bourdieu's theories, elaborated elsewhere in his work, of reading and reflexivity. Yet in a piece devoted to these themes, and in particular to the challenging of unconsciously 'scholastic' intellectual projections, Speller finds Bourdieu prone to projections of his own. The sociologist sees the text as a kind of device that demonstrates his own theory of habitus, and in his enthusiasm, perhaps, to find in Faulkner a support for his own sociological theory, he flattens the literary complexity of Faulkner's short story (neglecting notably the techniques of foreshadowing, imagery, and diffuse Gothic convention on which the author plays). Thus, while Speller concludes that this apparently anomalous chapter at the end of *The Rules* can in fact be integrated into the overall economy of Bourdieu's theory of literature, he also challenges the clear-cut opposition between 'naïve' and 'scholastic' readings which structures it.

Jeremy Ahearne begins his article with Bourdieu's stark critique from the 1960s of the role of literary education in reproducing social structures—a critique that led, correctly in some respects, to the charge of social reductionism, and to Bourdieu's reputation as an inveterate 'enemy' of literary culture and pedagogy. This was arguably reinforced by the the 'hypercontextualizing' imperative that Ahearne notes in Bourdieu's theory of the literary field, which, to avoid the 'fetishistic' investment in works and the premature 'universalizing' of readings, demands not only that literary texts be situated in multiple 'fields' and 'spaces', but also that the reader should submit him- or herself to an auto-analysis of his or her own 'position' and 'trajectory'—a seemingly unending process of successive 'double historicizations'. For all the undoubted advances in understanding thereby produced, these 'hypercontextualizing' injunctions nonetheless, Ahearne argues, risk stifling ordinary reading practices and the practical pedagogy of canon-formation. Moreover, Ahearne shows that Bourdieu's actual attitude towards literature and his own real practice belie his more one-sided perspectives and pronouncements. Taking the example of Bourdieu's long-term engagement with Blaise Pascal, Ahearne demonstrates how the sociologist inserts decontextualized fragments or 'shards' of literary text into his works. These enable him not only to express his ideas in a more arresting or even 'brutal' manner, but also to negotiate an experiential residue or excess encountered in his writing and that resists proper 'scientific' treatment. Literature, then, even or indeed sometimes especially when decontextualized, can be instructive. Moreover, Ahearne argues, Bourdieu's appropriation of Pascal itself leaves behind a revealing residue, which brings into focus blind spots in Bourdieu's thought (notably regarding his 'investment' in the world of science).

In 'On an Enigmatic Text by Pierre Bourdieu', Jérôme David begins by describing the feeling of perplexity that struck him upon first reading what is, to all intents and purposes, an *explication de texte* by Bourdieu of the Apollinaire poem 'Automne malade', dating from 1995 but written in the manner of a French professor or a particularly accomplished student from the 1950s. Even Bourdieu's use of a common term in his lexicon, *amor fati*, does not take him, David argues, into the realm of sociological analysis. Bourdieu's commentary appears to be an anachronism, not simply in terms of literary fashions, but also in the context of his wider work on literature, which had been strongly set against all forms of purely 'internalist', 'scholastic' reading. Yet rather than just a curiosity, David sees this commentary as revealing something about Bourdieu's intellectual and affective system (his habitus), specifically the range of possible relations he held with literature simultaneously and at different moments. In 'Apollinaire, Autumn Ill', a remnant from Bourdieu's scholastic unconscious re-emerges, and he enters into what David terms an 'ethical' relation to literature in which the reader is absorbed in a dialogue with the logic and internal dynamic of the work in itself. Bourdieu takes from the poem the same lesson the poet both draws from autumn and addresses to autumn: to accept and even love one's fate, *amor amoris fati*, up to and including one's demise and death. This was a surrender to nature, David argues, that Bourdieu's sociology would not have allowed him to deliver, but which, possibly with the prospect of his own death already on the horizon, he found the means to express in poetic language and literary analysis.

In a recently published collection in French entitled *Bourdieu et la littérature*, Jean-Pierre Martin recounts how he frequently asks amphitheatres full of literature students whether they have read any Bourdieu, and receives only a feeble showing of hands.[7] One can imagine a similar situation outside France. Meanwhile, in the many general books and introductions on Bourdieu, his work on literature has likewise been given little attention. Yet interest does appear to have grown, as literary researchers around the world appreciate the possibilities Bourdieu's theory offers for situating works historically and within the fields of production and reception, including in a transnational perspective; and as sociologists realize that literature for Bourdieu was more than just a sideline — that it was a core interest, inspiration and influence in his œuvre. In this special issue, seven scholars from different academic traditions and disciplines, working with and on Bourdieu in a variety of contexts and for a variety of purposes, provide a range of perspectives on Bourdieu's approaches to literature and the literary field, in theory and in practice. The result is a collective reappraisal of this underexamined but central component in his work, and in the intellectual habitus that generated it. At the same time, this issue may serve as a starting point for further 'Bourdieusian' research, and for continuing adaptation and refinement of his general theory of fields, including his specific theory of the literary field.

NOTES

1   See, for example, Pierre Bourdieu and Jean-Claude Passeron, *Reproduction in Education, Society and Culture* [1970], translated by Richard Nice (London: Sage, 1977); Pierre Bourdieu and Alain Darbel, *The Love of Art: European Art Museums and their Public* [1966], translated by Caroline Beattie and Nick Merriman (Cambridge: Polity, 1990); Bourdieu, *Language and Symbolic Power*, edited by John B. Thompson, translated by Gino Raymond and Matthew Adamson (Cambridge: Polity, 1991); Bourdieu, *The State Nobility: Elite Schools in the Field of Power* [1989], translated by Lauretta C. Clough (Cambridge: Polity, 1996); Bourdieu, *The Political Ontology of Martin Heidegger* [1988], translated by Peter Collier (Cambridge: Polity, 1991); Bourdieu, *On Television*

and Journalism [1996], translated by Priscilla Parkhurst Ferguson (London: Pluto, 1998); Bourdieu, *The Social Structures of the Economy* [2000], translated by Chris Turner (Cambridge: Polity, 2005).

2 Bourdieu himself would come to see some of his more aggressive phrasing as counterproductive (see, for example, specifically in relation to literature, the comments on his earlier 'needless excesses' ('outrances inutiles'), in Bourdieu, *The Rules of Art: Genesis and Structure of the Literary Field* [1992], translated by Susan Emanuel (Cambridge: Polity, 1996), 185). Nonetheless, more generally, the very resistance to the terms of Bourdieu's analyses within different fields was often integrated by Bourdieu into subsequent analyses as yielding significant insight into those fields.

3 See Jean-Pierre Martin, 'Avant-propos: Bourdieu le désenchanteur' in *Bourdieu et la littérature*, edited by Jean-Pierre Martin (Nantes: Editions Cécile Defaut, 2010), 7–21.

4 Pierre Bourdieu, *Esquisse pour une auto-analyse* (Paris: Raisons d'agir, 2004), 87.

5 Pierre Bourdieu, 'Champ intellectuel et projet créateur', *Les Temps modernes* 246 (1966), 865–906; and Pierre Bourdieu, 'Une révolution conservatrice dans l'édition', *Actes de la Recherche en Sciences Sociales* 126–7 (1999), 3–28.

6 Pierre Bourdieu, 'Apollinaire, Automne malade', *Cahiers d'Histoire des littératures romanes /Romanistische Zeitschrift für Literaturgeschichte* 3–4 (1995), 330–3, translated in this volume.

7 Jean-Pierre Martin, 'Avant-propos, Bourdieu le désenchanteur', 7.

How Field Theory Can Contribute to Knowledge of World Literary Space

ANNA BOSCHETTI

Abstract:
Anglophone scholars with a postcolonial perspective have forcefully challenged eurocentric definitions of comparative literature and the limits of national frameworks. But this debate 'offers few methodological solutions to the pragmatic issue of how to make credible comparisons among radically different languages and literatures' (Emily Apter). Moreover, some have even rejected the very notion of comparison, impugning its association with nationalistic and imperialistic perspectives or its unsuitability for the study of historical, dynamic and multidimensional processes. This article offers a synthetic overview of the tools field theory provides for literature studies in a global perspective without sacrificing methodological rigour and empirical validation. It discusses the epistemological principles set out in *The Craft of Sociology* to address problems of comparison; the possibility of rational dialogue between different theoretical frameworks; the properties which make Bourdieu's model more complete than other approaches to literary phenomena; and finally, developments of field theory and issues raised by globalization.

Keywords: Pierre Bourdieu, literature, globalization, field theory

This article focuses on the conceptual tools and empirical examples found in Bourdieu's work and in research inspired by his field theory on literature in a worldwide perspective. To account for Bourdieu's theoretical research, I will situate it in the space of contemporary approaches to culture and underline how some developments of his theory have been stimulated by other frameworks. As the history of science shows, the dialogue between seemingly distant disciplinary areas is a key condition for progress in knowledge,[1] and the

Paragraph 35.1 (2012): 10–29
DOI: 10.3366/para.2012.0039
© Edinburgh University Press
www.eupjournals.com/para

formulation of new laws is generally a result of the effort to explain and reconcile different existing theories.[2]

Anglophone scholars have contributed decisively to questioning the premises and methods of literary history. Cultural studies, for instance, has promoted an anti-disciplinary way of thinking.[3] This attitude risks slipping into eclecticism and impressionism, but it helps scholars to go beyond mental boundaries, which constitute an obstacle to cognitive progress. Labels such as 'imagined community',[4] 'cosmopolitanism',[5] 'world literature',[6] 'postcolonial' and 'diaspora' studies, or 'transnationalism', are responses to the need for a rejection of national perspectives and elaboration of new theoretical tools. They have also questioned the classical Marxist approach to society and culture: it is not enough to consider class position, since many other social differences — ethnicity, religion, politics, language, gender and so on — can play an important role. These researchers have underlined the mobility of cultural phenomena: people, books and ideas circulate, and in the process change and contribute to producing changes in literature and society. Postcolonial theorists have stressed processes of hybridization and transformation rather than oppositions between cultural traditions.

But, as Emily Apter has argued, this debate 'offers few method-ological solutions to the pragmatic issue of how to make credible comparisons among radically different languages and literatures'.[7] Several scholars in the USA and in Europe have gone so far as to reject the very notion of comparison. Susan Bassnett declared fifteen years ago: 'Today, comparative literature in one sense is dead.'[8] And Gayatri Chakravorty Spivak gave her book on this subject the title *Death of a Discipline*.[9] For some authors, comparison is associated with a nationalistic and imperialistic point of view.[10] For others, comparison is not suitable for the study of historical, dynamic and multidimensional phenomena.[11]

The Conditions of a Reflexive Comparatism

Bourdieu's work provides tools to address the problems of rational dialogue among different theories and methods. I refer in particular to a book that is forty-three years old but still valid, *Le Métier de sociologue*, written by Bourdieu with Jean-Claude Passeron and Jean-Claude Chamboredon, published in French in 1968 and translated into English in 1991 with the title *The Craft of Sociology*.[12] The main goal of this book is to set out the epistemological principles that should be respected so as to make comparison and integration of results possible in the social sciences. According to these principles, it does not make sense to reject comparison, since it is a constituent dimension of any act of knowledge. It is comparison that allows us to formulate general concepts. Even the simplest form of classification, everyday concepts such as table, house or cat, presupposes a comparison of many different cases. This is why Durkheim claims that 'comparative sociology is not a particular branch of sociology; it is sociology itself, in so far as it ceases to be purely descriptive and aspires to account for facts'.[13]

Nevertheless, comparison is difficult in the social sciences.[14] In practice, it is too often a bad comparison, reduced to a two-term opposition, as if social objects were essences outside time and not overlapping and constantly evolving processes. One of the main problems, in comparison as in any cognitive operation, is the positivist attitude, which ignores the constructivist dimension of knowledge. Implicitly, positivism presupposes that spontaneous empirical observation can by itself reach an objective view of reality. Positivism leads us to take for granted our mental schemes and to ignore the effects of bias produced by the fact that any observer has a particular 'point of view' shaped by his or her own trajectory.

Language is the main vector of mental categories. So, to break with false notions we need first of all to break with our linguistic habits. We have to analyse and historicize our concepts: not only the concepts of the individuals observed, but also the concepts we researchers use in our studies. So we have to retrace the genesis, uses and social stakes of concepts. And we have to pay particular attention to seemingly obvious concepts, such as literature, culture, civilization, nation, region and identity — not to mention the concepts used in literary history: classicism, romanticism, realism, avant-garde, modernity, futurism, post-modernism and so on, or genre classifications, such as poetry, drama and the novel.[15]

Most current approaches to culture are not far from this way of thinking. Currently, the role played by culture in building social reality has been brought to the fore. Many scholars assume, at least implicitly, that all social facts and representations are historical products. This means we cannot explain a social phenomenon without considering the historical processes that have generated it. We also have to consider the points of view of individuals, by reconstructing the particular geo-political and cultural configurations in which they are englobed. The world, at any particular moment in its history, has been the stage for many different configurations, processes, perceptions and 'modernities'. This idea has been captured by Reinhart Koselleck in his succinct formulation 'the nonsimultaneity of the simultaneous',[16] as well as by François Hartog, with his notion of 'regimes of historicity'.[17]

In short, many researchers from different traditions today appreciate the need to historicize concepts. I am not only referring here to the *Begriffsgeschichte* group,[18] the School of Cambridge[19] and the New Sociology of Ideas,[20] but, in general, to an increasing number of studies devoted to retracing the circulation of ideas, concepts and metaphors.[21] These convergences, it seems to me, are important steps towards a rational dialogue between different approaches to culture.

The Craft of Sociology also emphasizes the crucial role played by theoretical frameworks in the progress of knowledge. Moreover, this book indicates the main requirements for a good theory. For example, it should not be an *ad hoc* model, valid only for an individual case. It has to be a systematic and coherent body of hypotheses that can help us break with impressionistic explanations. A good theory should be transposable and every new application is a test of its validity. The slightest difficulty or contradiction can question the entire edifice and force its adjustment. A good theory is also a research programme: it has to guide the researcher in every step of his work. Moreover, it must make comparison possible between different objects, situated in various historical configurations, and allow us to produce studies that are comparative and comparable. Even an individual case study is, in fact, comparative, if we conceive of it as a methodical transfer of general hypotheses. In this way, a good case study can be a useful contribution to the collective and cumulative progress of knowledge.

I want to underline the importance of this point: it means that we can reconcile a rigorous analysis — by definition limited and circumscribed — with a worldwide perspective. The more we produce comparable studies, the more we can contribute to founding a new, scientific comparative literature. It will be possible to compare a great number of case studies, concerning very different objects,[22] without resigning ourselves to the 'distant reading' proposed by Franco Moretti, who argues that a single author cannot apply the methods of 'close reading' to the immense variety of cases presented by 'world literature'.[23] It is not through approximate maps that we can claim to account for this diversity. And we should not forget to historicize and question the notion of 'world literature' itself, if we wish to discover the implicit assumptions that lie behind its re-application.[24]

Situating Field Theory in the Space of Contemporary Approaches to Culture

In addition to these epistemological principles, Bourdieu also elaborated a general theoretical model which has been proven to be very powerful in its applications to literature.[25] To present his theory, we can begin with a main opposition that distinguishes it from more established theories in the anglophone tradition. Like Durkheim, Bourdieu thinks of society as a whole. Their approach, in other words, is holistic. This means that parts cannot be understood except in their relation to the whole. In contrast, the American tradition tends to explain society as the result of interactions between individuals. This perspective is shared, for instance, by Erving Goffman,[26] by so-called symbolic interactionism,[27] by various methods of network analysis and by the 'Chicago school'. A representative of this school, Howard Becker, has been one of the main references for American cultural studies.[28] Moreover, individualism and interactionism dominate many academic fields influenced by cultural studies and multiculturalism, in particular anthropology and science and technology studies.[29]

Of course, network analysis can be useful, and in fact many field studies integrate it.[30] But interactionism does not allow us to explain every aspect of social reality. The human world is not simply the result of interactions between individuals in the present, but the product of a long historical process. It is a stage already set when we enter upon it, so its structures and functioning contribute to shaping mental categories. Moreover, the probability that people interact and the ways in which they interact depend on social structures. We have to consider both the points of view of individuals and their actions. But we cannot explain practices without having reconstituted the structure of the social space and their positions within it.

The holistic approach is shared by many well-known thinkers such as Althusser, Foucault, Luhmann, Habermas, Itamar Even-Zohar and most exponents of Translation Studies, as well as by neo-Marxist authors such as Immanuel Wallerstein, Fredric Jameson, Abram De Swaan and David Harvey. But Bourdieu's framework is more integrated and complete than others, and provides literary studies with original and effective tools. The 'theory of practice' expressed by the concepts of habitus and field helps us to explain at once the coherence and diversity of perceptions and choices. The habitus is shaped by the conditions of existence and experiences associated with a particular social trajectory. Trajectories of socially close individuals generate similar habitus and conducts. At the same time, there are no two identical habitus, since trajectories are never identical. The concept of field is particularly interesting for research on literature, since it was initially conceived and developed to account for the specificity of literary practices.[31] Persuaded that the sociological tradition had not explored adequately the symbolic dimension of the social world, Bourdieu aimed to fill that gap. From the mid-sixties he regarded literature as a particularly significant object from this point of view, because it is a 'world reversed': a field in which a symbolic logic prevails while power relations and any form of interest (economic, political and symbolic) are denied and perceived as relations of meaning. Moreover, none of the existing approaches to literature was able satisfactorily to explain specific aspects such as the properties of texts, nor the great variety of ways of reading and evaluating them.

Bourdieu meditated on the work of his predecessors concerning the implications of the process of division of labour. He was particularly impressed by Weber's analysis of ancient Judaism, which showed that one cannot understand the practices of agents — priests, prophets, magicians — specialized in producing religious goods without taking into account their positions and their competitive relations.[32] The concept of field elaborates and systematizes these suggestions in an original way: to the extent that a human activity is specialized, it tends to organize itself as a microcosm characterized by its own way of functioning. To understand what happens in a field one should therefore consider its specific logic: stakes, values, forms of symbolic capital, hierarchies, techniques, institutions and (essential for the functioning of the 'game') what Bourdieu calls '*illusio*', a Latin term signifying the total involvement of players in a social game. Each field has its own forms of '*illusio*', 'interest' and 'capital': what is important for a poet does not have the same value for a geographer and vice versa.

This process of specialization has various effects. First, it creates what Bourdieu describes as a 'space of possibilities', a repertoire of models which changes constantly. With regard to the literary field, the 'possibilities' are genres, themes, techniques, styles, institutions and different material supports. They are also representations of literature, of writers and other figures such as publishers and critics. The meaning and value of each option depends on the state of the literary field: the choice of free verse, which was original and daring in the 1880s, seemed trivial two decades later. Field theory takes into account not only the processes of production, but also the mechanisms of diffusion and legitimation of literary works, showing how it is possible to understand their 'reception' and the value attributed to them, through a methodical reconstruction of the collective process by which they are produced. Literature is characterized by its own forms of socializing, which are at the same time strategies of alliance, more or less institutionalized or informal, open or closed: academies, salons, clubs, cafés, groups. We must also consider agents and institutions upon which the publication and the consecration of works depend (publishers, literary agents, reviews, critics, translators), without forgetting the action of the school system, which can canonize works by including them in its programmes, and can transform students into competent and passionate readers by providing them with appropriate skills of perception and evaluation.

Bourdieu underlines the great difference between his challenging research programme and reception theories which conceive of the act of reading as an intuitive comprehension, which affirm that it is guided by the texts themselves with reference to an 'implicit reader',[33] or which stress the 'reader's creativity', which could somehow escape the control of 'interpretative communities'[34] or the literary 'institution'.[35] According to Bourdieu, freedom and intuition are likely to be but seductive illusions, if we do not analyse the concrete empirical ways through which social determinations, such as schemes of perception, limit the subject's point of view.

Bourdieu's model assigns key importance to agents and the competition between them. Each agent (author, publisher, critic, scholar) tends in fact to pursue and promote his or her own conception of literature, which depends both on that agent's habitus and on the material and/or symbolic interests associated with his or her position. To indicate the fact that these choices are not random, Bourdieu uses the term 'strategy', the sense of which differs in his theory from common usage. It does not imply that action is based on the conscious pursuit of profit. The case of writers provides a good example of this: while there may be some agents who do try deliberately to adapt their products to market demand, others are guided spontaneously by their perception of the game and consider their choices to be totally disinterested, in accordance with the fundamental *nomos* of the literary field. As a result of competition, the literary field functions as an objectively structured space, differentiated and hierarchical in all its aspects (although, being the object of struggle, hierarchies can change at any time). The 'legitimacy' of each position depends on its 'symbolic capital': the recognition of a small circle formed by the most prestigious writers, publishers, critics and institutions active in the field. In more autonomous fields this hierarchy is opposed to that based on commercial profit, to the extent that market success can discredit an author in the eyes of 'legitimate' producers and their readers.

The field exercises a 'prism effect' on all external determinations and refracts them according to its own logic. Thus, literary practices cannot satisfactorily be explained through a biography, which treats them as direct expressions of personal experiences and feelings. Marxist approaches also commit a 'short circuit', either by considering cultural products as a mirror of power relations between social classes (as Georg Lukács and Lucien Goldmann do), or by only taking into account markets. The positions occupied by agents in the field are, according to Bourdieu, the most important explanatory factor, since writers are guided in their work and even in their lifestyles by the opportunities the field offers them, given the properties of their positions. Bourdieu describes the relation between agents and the field as the encounter between two relatively independent 'histories': the trajectory of the individual and the history of the field. To understand literary practices we have to reconstitute both histories and their encounter, combining macro- and microanalysis to consider all factors that explain the different trajectories, representations and choices of agents. Feelings of affinity or incompatibility towards other agents and their products depend on objective relations of proximity or distance between the respective positions: whether they are avant-garde, traditional writers, stars of bourgeois salons, or popular authors. Agents make choices more or less suited to their positions, according to the degrees to which they are integrated into literary life and have developed a practical mastery of its functioning.

The determining role attributed to agents and to their competitive relationships is one of the main differences that distinguishes Bourdieu's theory from other approaches to literature. Formalist frameworks, by definition, do not take agents into account. Even Michel Foucault, though he recognized, as Bourdieu does, the historicity of 'symbolic forms', did not explain the passage from one configuration to another, nor the diversity of practices that can be observed in the same historical 'episteme', since he refused explicitly to consider agents, their trajectories, their specific interests and their struggles.[36] None of the frameworks based on the concept of system proposes a theory of action remotely comparable to Bourdieu's model in its ability to explain the variety of representations and practices that may be classified as literature.

Moreover, far from reducing the social world to a model of mechanical self-reproduction, as its detractors claim, field theory offers very useful tools with which to account for crises and changes. As a literary microcosm is never completely independent of the social space in which it is included, to explain its history it is not enough to consider internal factors such as competition among producers. The increasing mobility and complexity of the social world could not fail to have affected literature, albeit indirectly. It is therefore necessary to pay attention not only to the relations between the literary field and the various forms of power (political, economic, religious) that can interfere with it, but also to the evolution of the cultural space as a whole. Changes in literature (status, way of functioning, canons) are intimately connected with transformations of the galaxy of various, variable and relatively independent microcosms that produce culture: printed works, arts, audiovisual media, more or less disciplinarized forms of knowledge, education.[37] The interactions between these sectors are not anarchic, they are structured by power relations. The impact each produces also depends on the materials and techniques they employ.

This view is very distant from that of authors such as Homi Bahbha[38] and Arjun Appadurai.[39] These authors tend to reject the structural analysis of geo-political, cultural and linguistic hierarchies. According to these authors, this kind of analysis reinforces nationalistic and essentialist modes of thinking. Thus, they point to the positive effects of mobility and to the active role played by agents. According to Bourdieu, it is precisely when we misunderstand power relations inscribed in the structure of the social world that we allow 'symbolic violence' to act without restraint. And we cannot explain cultural practices without reconstituting social divisions and hierarchies, since these have important effects on people's minds and on their behaviours. One needs only think of the influence that American culture has had over the imagination of people all over the planet, through cinema, radio, advertizing, TV and the internet. So the wonderful freedom that Appadurai attributes to the imagination is likely to be wishful thinking, and risks reinforcing cultural imperialism.

In a chapter of *The Rules of Art* Bourdieu gives an explicit form to his model. According to *The Craft of Sociology*, to render hypotheses explicit is an important step in theoretical construction: it is a way to systematize the theory and allow others to use and verify it. Bourdieu's model is, in fact, an *ars inveniendi*, which can help scholars to identify relevant data and operations, as well as to see relations between facts that are generally studied separately. Since it requires the researcher to consider not only the processes of production and consecration in all their aspects, but also the complex cultural and geo-political system in which literature is situated, it has decompartmentalized the study of literature and opened up new directions for research, involving sociology and the history of culture. Bourdieu did not have time to write about the relationship between literature and other cultural fields, aside from some remarks concerning exchanges with painting[40] and the power exercised by journalism[41] and publishing.[42] This is a very promising avenue for research, which could radically renew literary history. Already some work has highlighted, for example, that publishing, translation and journalism can contribute to stimulating literary innovation.[43] The great changes taking place today in publishing and in the intermedia system are certainly having important effects on literature, which remain largely unexplored.[44]

A Collective Work in Progress

The results of scientific research are by definition provisional and subject to revision. And, as the authors of *The Craft of Sociology* remind us, quoting Bachelard, one of the main ways in which knowledge can progress is through the effort to understand the logic of error, and by submitting our hypotheses and practices to methodical and permanent correction. So it is useful to recall some weaknesses and risks which emerge in Bourdieu's own work and in studies inspired by Bourdieu. These problems, it seems to me, do not disqualify Bourdieu's theory, but do question some applications of it. It is therefore worth mentioning them, since they can become starting points for new directions and developments in research.

Some of my concerns refer to the first chapter of *The Rules of Art*, where Bourdieu sets himself a very demanding goal: he tries to trace the development of the French literary field over a long period in its history. I think we should read this text as a first draft that strives to present its object as a whole, rather than as a systematic empirical analysis. But, if we want to progress, we should also recognize its gaps and limitations. For instance, Bourdieu does not question many of the legacies of traditional literary history, such as the national perspective. Of course, it is impossible to rethink every notion inherited from the past, especially in an initial analysis. Bourdieu himself indicated, later on, how his model could be transposed to the global scale, so as to situate every local fact—national and regional—in the increasingly complex and variable system of relations formed by geo-political spaces and fields engendered by the division of labour.[45] He also underlined the need to take into account the specific meanings that texts assume, according to the national contexts and intellectual traditions in which they circulate.[46]

The most questionable aspect in this first attempt at historical synthesis appears when Bourdieu naturalizes the concept of field and seems to forget that it is only a theoretical tool which he uses to describe the functioning of social worlds. Sometimes he speaks of the field as if it were an empirical phenomenon, with a precise place and date of birth: France at the time of Flaubert and Baudelaire. So he risks committing the same mistake for which he criticizes other authors, such as Lévi-Strauss and Weber: he takes a notion for a historical reality.[47] This naturalization has regrettable consequences, since several scholars have tended to reproduce it, by taking Bourdieu's reconstruction for a general definition, as if we could use the concept of field only for a literary space as autonomous as the French field was, according to Bourdieu, around 1850. If we think of fields as really existent objects we risk raising false problems, such as the question of whether Belgian writers constitute a field.[48] It would be better and simpler to wonder if in our objects there are aspects that could be explained using field theory. Thus, Alain Viala and Olivier Christin have applied the notion of field to the seventeenth century,[49] and Robert Darnton, Roger Chartier, Daniel Roche to the eighteenth century. I think we could also use it profitably to study more distant periods, such as some aspects of culture in ancient Greece.

In one of his early papers, 'The Market of Symbolic Goods', Bourdieu stressed the relationship between the autonomization of the literary field and the growth of the market.[50] But *The Rules of Art* is more focused on the process of autonomization. So it concentrates on canonical literature, and pays little regard to the market and its influence on the selection and canonization of works. Most other field studies, including my own books on Sartre and Apollinaire, do the same.[51] No doubt, this trend is partly due to strong disciplinary habits, and it implies many risks. For instance, we risk falling into a normative attitude by taking canons, which are the products of past struggles, for value judgements. We could also end up treating legitimate literature as if it were a totally autonomous reality, just as traditional literary studies do. Such risks are not completely avoided in *The World Republic of Letters* by Pascale Casanova, a book which marks, however, significant progress, since it was the first application of Bourdieu's model on a planetary scale.[52] Due to the immensity of the task it is difficult to escape simplification. For example, Casanova's framework is based on the idea of a singular historical time and of a singular modernity: the evolution of canons seems to depend on only one dominant tradition. Moreover, Casanova tends to focus only on legitimate literature and to ignore commercial production, as well as the market and other factors that play a role in literary history. She also has a tendency to idealize the verdicts of the 'World Republic of Letters', as if these were a guarantee of value. Indeed, various empirical analyses have shown that so-called 'pure Literature' is not naturally cosmopolitan and universalist, nor separable from the history of commercial products and consumptions.[53]

Cultural studies, meanwhile, has brought popular and mass culture to the fore, but ended up by forgetting literature. So, on both sides of the Channel, very few authors have tried to reconstruct the functioning of culture as a whole. I would like to mention some important exceptions, such as Christophe Charle. Very early on, he saw the need to carry out comparative studies embracing the European space.[54] His books focus not only on literature, but also on genres such as theatre and opera, and he takes into account the market, publishing, the public, criticism, media, as well as other important dimensions of intellectual history, such as the education of the elite,[55] the evolution of academic fields and disciplines,[56] the field of power and the role of ideologies.[57]

Charle and other scholars have clarified an often misunderstood aspect of field theory, concerning the relationship between politics and literature. According to Bourdieu, autonomy does not mean an apolitical attitude. And a political position or intent does not imply, per se, the author's heteronomy. This is the case only for works that are subordinate to political demand. This point is highlighted by Gisèle Sapiro and Ioana Popa in their studies of authoritarian regimes, in which all texts, even apolitical ones, take on a political meaning. But writers who look for the approval of political power have positions and practices which are very different from writers who hold independent political opinions.[58]

Field Theory and Globalization

Recent applications and developments of field theory have sought to address issues raised by globalization. The national point of view has been thrown into question by studies that apply the notion of field to different configurations: polycentric traditions, federal and/or multilingual countries, little regional enclaves, supranational linguistic or ethnic areas, postcolonial countries. It has become recognized that researchers need to vary the scale of analysis from the supranational to the infranational level. Some works have underlined the decisive role played by Paris and other capital cities in the history of culture.[59] Others have shown that the building of nations is always a transnational process,[60] in which nationalism and cosmopolitanism are far from mutually exclusive.[61] Several analyses have highlighted the importance of ethnic and religious affinities in intellectual history. Most of these studies pay more attention to dynamic aspects, such as processes of circulation, as well as to tensions and transformations produced by mobility.[62] Works on translation and other forms of cultural transfer combine statistical methods and microanalysis to bring out the complexity of the stakes and factors shaping relationships among different cultures and/or languages.[63] Moreover, there has been an increasing interest in the comparison of different approaches and traditions.[64] This is the only way for a theoretical framework to avoid dogmatism and remain 'progressive', to use Imre Lakatos's term.[65] This evolution has been stimulated, in particular, by dialogue with anglophone scholars.

Concluding Remarks

Thanks to the internationalization of research, many scholars now appreciate the need to make dialogue between researchers and the integration of results possible, to account for the great diversity of literary phenomena in the world. Contrary to what some scholars have claimed, the failure of the traditional comparative approach does not require a rejection of the notion of comparison, but obliges us to reconsider the conditions for credible and fruitful comparisons, which may contribute to founding a transnational and global vision of literary history.

   Although people who study literature are sometimes suspicious of theory and convinced that they can do without it, any analysis in fact implies a theory, a vision of reality and knowledge, because our minds do not have immediate access to things, but perceive them according to categories, which may be more or less adequate. So theoretical reflexivity has an extremely important role in research. Pierre Bourdieu's work offers very helpful tools from this point of view. Firstly, in the *The Craft of Sociology* and other writings he formulated the basic principles that all human sciences (including literary studies) should respect if they want to enable empirical verification and comparison of their findings. He also indicates how to achieve a posture of epistemological vigilance: for example, by historicizing concepts, an essential weapon against automatisms of language and thought. We should apply this reflexive approach to all the concepts we have inherited from literary history, beginning with the very notions of literature, poetry and the novel.

Moreover, Bourdieu elaborated a complex and systematic theory of society, centred on the concepts of habitus and field, which opens new and fruitful perspectives on the study of literature. This model is inspired partly by structuralism, as it not only explains individual choices as a result of interactions, but also takes into account the structure of the space in which agents are situated. Yet, unlike structuralism and the various theories based on the concept of system, Bourdieu's theory takes the subjective side of action and history into account. The concept of field explains the more specific aspects of literary phenomena as effects of a process of autonomization and specialization. Literature, like many other human activities, developed over time as a microcosm with its own way of functioning: challenges, techniques, institutions, representations, hierarchies, values, forms of capital and interest, mechanisms of publication and consecration. So, to explain a literary fact it is necessary to reconstruct the state of the literary field at the moment of its production.

Agents and the competition between them are of particular importance in Bourdieu's model and this fact distinguishes it from most other theories. Formalist frameworks tend not even to take agents into account, while biographies and traditional Marxist approaches (Lukács, Adorno, Goldmann) commit a 'short circuit' error, according to Bourdieu, when they try to explain properties of literary works directly as effects of the experiences of individuals, or as 'reflections' of economic power relationships. If no field is totally independent of the structure of the space in which it is included, its specific logic acts like a prism, re-translating any external determination. Everyone involved in literary life (authors, publishers, critics, translators) is guided in their choices by a 'point of view', which depends mainly on their relative positions in the field. Bourdieu's method requires that we should also pay close attention to the agents and institutions involved in the circulation and legitimization of works, such as publishing and criticism, not to mention the school system, which not only transmits literary canons but also educates and creates a public for 'high' literature.

Contrary to the criticism that Bourdieu's models give an image of static formations condemned to reproduce existing structures, field theory provides tools for thinking about change in literary forms and canons. The key factor is internal competition between agents, in particular the need for new entrants to challenge established positions. Transformations of the surrounding space may help internal changes indirectly, although it would be wrong to treat them as direct 'causes' or principles of explanation. In addition to political or economic crises, researchers should consider the variable power relations between different fields of cultural production. Increasing globalization as well as the evolution of technology, media, education systems and academic disciplines cannot fail to have important effects on literature.

In *The Rules of Art*, Bourdieu not only set out theoretical principles and a research programme, but also provided an empirical example: a history of the French literary field, beginning in the middle of the nineteenth century. His reconstruction proves the heuristic power of his hypotheses and, if it is not without questionable aspects (like any pioneering enterprise), these do not concern the theoretical principles but rather their application. For example, Bourdieu remains anchored to a national perspective and tends to naturalize the concept of field. Moreover, *The Rules of Art* and several studies inspired by Bourdieu's model are focused on high literature, a choice that can have a distorting effect as it distracts from the role of mass production in the transformation of literature. But many other more recent applications have shown that the model is transposable to any kind of literary tradition and work. On one hand, *The World Republic of Letters* by Pascale Casanova has applied Bourdieu's framework to a worldwide perspective, opening the way for many other studies that apply field theory to understand transnational dynamics. These works sometimes integrate the findings and approaches of different disciplines, such as Cultural Studies and Translation Studies, which stress hybridization effects and tensions arising from the mobility of works and producers. On the other hand, there is an increasing attention to the role that transformations in the market, press, technology and media can play in literary changes.

NOTES

1   See for example Mattei Dogan, Robert Pahre, *Creative Marginality. Innovation at the Intersection of the Sciences* (Boulder, CO: Westview, 1990); Johan Heilbron, 'Regime of Disciplines: Toward an Historical Sociology of

Disciplinary Knowledge', in *The Dialogical Turn: New Roles for Sociology in the Postdisciplinary Age*, edited by Charles Camic and Hans Joas (Lanham, MD: Rowman & Littlefield, 2004), 23–42.

2 Norman Campbell, *What is Science?* (London: Methuen, 1921), 88.

3 See Stéphane Van Damme, 'Comprendre les *Cultural Studies*: une approche d'histoire des savoirs', *Revue d'Histoire moderne et contemporaine* 51:4 (2004), 48–58 (56).

4 Benedict Anderson, *Imagined Communities. Reflections on the Origin and Spread of Nationalism* (London: Verso, 1983).

5 Timothy Brennan, *At Home in the World: Cosmopolitanism Now* (Cambridge, MA: Harvard University Press, 1997); *Cosmopolitics. Thinking and Feeling beyond the Nation*, edited by Pheng Cheah and Bruce Robbins (Minneapolis: University of Minnesota Press, 1998).

6 David Damrosch, *What is World Literature?* (Princeton: Princeton University Press, 2003).

7 Emily Apter, 'Global *Translatio*. The "Invention" of Comparative Literature, Istanbul, 1933', *Critical Inquiry* 29:2 (Winter 2003), 253–81 (255).

8 Susan Bassnett, *Comparative Literature. A Critical Introduction* (Oxford: Blackwell, 1993), 47.

9 Gayatri Chakravorty Spivak, *Death of a Discipline* (New York: Columbia University Press, 2003).

10 Harry Harootunian, 'Ghostly Comparisons: Anderson's Telescope', *Diacritics* 29:4 (1999), 135–49 (146).

11 *De la comparaison à l'histoire croisée*, edited by Michael Werner and Bénédicte Zimmermann (Paris: Seuil, 2004), 17.

12 Pierre Bourdieu, Jean-Claude Passeron and Jean-Claude Chamboredon, *The Craft of Sociology* [1968], translated by Richard Nice (New York: Walter de Gruyter, 1991).

13 Emile Durkheim, *The Division of Labor in Society* [1893], Book 1, Ch. 2, translated by George Simpson (Glencoe, IL: The Free Press, 1949), 139.

14 See Neil J. Smelser, 'On Comparative Analysis, Interdisciplinarity and Internationalization in Sociology', *International Sociology* 18:4 (2003), 643–57.

15 See Christophe Charle, 'L'habitus scholastique et ses effets: à propos des classifications littéraires et historiques', in *L'Inconscient académique*, edited by F. Clément et al. (Geneva/Zurich: Editions Seismo, 2006), 67–87.

16 Reinhart Koselleck, *The Practice of Conceptual History: Timing History, Spacing Concepts* (Stanford: Stanford University Press, 2002), 8.

17 François Hartog, *Régimes d'historicité. Présentisme et expériences du temps* (Paris: Seuil, 2003).

18 *Geschichtliche Grundbegriffe: Historisches Lexikon zur politisch-sozialen Sprache*, 8 vols., edited by Otto Brunner, Werner Conze and Reinhart Koselleck (Stuttgart: Klett-Cotta, 1972–97).

19   *Political Innovation and Conceptual Change*, edited by Terence Ball, James Farr and Russel L. Hanson (Cambridge: Cambridge University Press, 1989); Quentin Skinner, 'The Idea of a Cultural Lexicon', *Essays in Criticism* 29 (1979) 205–24 and *Regarding Method*, Vol. I of *Visions of Politics*, 3 vols (London: Routledge, 2002), 158–74.

20   Charles Camic and Neil Gross, 'The New Sociology of Ideas', in *The Blackwell Companion to Sociology*, edited by J. R. Blau (Oxford: Blackwell, 2004).

21   See for example *Dictionnaire des concepts nomades en sciences humaines*, edited by Olivier Christin (Paris: Métailié, 2010).

22   See for example *L'Espace intellectuel en Europe: De la formation des États-nations à la mondialisation, XIXᵉ–XXᵉ siècles*, edited by Gisèle Sapiro (Paris: La Découverte, 2009); *L'Espace culturel transnational*, edited by Anna Boschetti (Paris: Nouveau Monde, 2010); *Dictionnaire des concepts nomades en sciences humaines*, edited by Olivier Christin.

23   Franco Moretti, 'Conjectures on World Literature', *New Left Review* 1 (2000), 54–68.

24   See Xavier Landrin, 'La sémantique historique de la *Weltliteratur*: genèse conceptuelle et usages savants', in *L'Espace culturel transnational*, edited by Anna Boschetti, 73–134.

25   Presentations of Bourdieu's anthropological theory can be found, in particular, in the following books: *Outline of a Theory of Practice*, translated by Richard Nice (Cambridge: Cambridge University Press, 1977); *Distinction. A Social Critique of the Judgement of Taste*, translated by Richard Nice (Cambridge, MA: Harvard University Press, 1984); *Pascalian Meditations,* translated by Richard Nice (Cambridge: Polity Press, 2000). See also Pierre Bourdieu and Loïc Wacquant, *An Invitation to Reflexive Sociology* (Chicago/Cambridge: University of Chicago Press/Polity Press, 1992).

26   Erving Goffman, *The Presentation of Self in Everyday Life* (Edinburgh: University of Edinburgh, 1959).

27   See Herbert Blumer, *Symbolic Interactionism. Perspective and Method* (Berkeley: University of California Press, 1969).

28   Howard Becker, *Outsiders* (Glencoe: Free Press/Macmillan Publishing Co., 1963).

29   See for example Bruno Latour, *Reassembling the Social: An Introduction to Actor-Network-Theory* (Oxford: Oxford University Press, 2005).

30   See Gisèle Sapiro, 'Réseaux, institution(s) et champ', in *Les Réseaux littéraires*, edited by Daphne de Marneffe and Benoît Denis (Bruxelles: Le CRI/CIEL, 2006), 44–59.

31   The first text in which Bourdieu uses the concept of field is about literature: Pierre Bourdieu, 'Champ intellectuel et projet créateur', *Les Temps modernes* 246 (1966), 865–906. Bourdieu presents a more elaborated and systematic version of field theory in his book on literature and art *The Rules of*

Art: Genesis and Structure of the Literary Field [1992], translated by Susan Emanuel (Cambridge: Polity Press, 1996).

32 See Max Weber, *Ancient Judaism*, translated and edited by Hans H. Gerth and Don Martindale (New York: The Free Press, 1967). See also the articles where Bourdieu presents his interpretation of Weberian analysis and applies the concept of field to religion: Pierre Bourdieu, 'Une interprétation de la théorie de la religion selon Max Weber', *Archives européennes de sociologie* 12:1 (1971), 3–21; 'Genèse et structure du champ religieux', *Revue française de sociologie* 12:3 (1971), 295–334.

33 Wolfgang Iser, *The Act of Reading. A Theory of Aesthetic Response* (Baltimore: Johns Hopkins University Press, 1978); Umberto Eco, *The Role of the Reader. Explorations in the Semiotics of Texts*, edited by Thomas Sebeok (Bloomington: Indiana University Press, 1979).

34 Stanley E. Fish, *Is There a Text in This Class? The Authority of Interpretive Communities* (Cambridge, MA: Harvard University Press, 1980).

35 Michel de Certeau, *The Practice of Everyday Life*, translated by Steven Rendall (Berkeley: University of California Press, 1984).

36 See Michel Foucault, 'Réponse au cercle d'épistémologie', *Cahiers pour l'analyse* 9 (1968), 9–40.

37 See Anna Boschetti, 'L'explication du changement', in *Bourdieu et la littérature*, edited by Jean-Pierre Martin (Nantes: Cécile Defaut, 2010), 93–111.

38 Homi K. Bhabha, *The Location of Culture* (London and New York: Routledge, 1994).

39 Arjun Appadurai, *Modernity at Large: Cultural Dimensions of Globalization* (Minneapolis: University of Minnesota Press, 1996).

40 See *The Rules of Art*, Ch. 2.

41 Pierre Bourdieu, *On Television and Journalism*, translated by Priscilla Parkhust Ferguson (London: Pluto, 1998).

42 Pierre Bourdieu, 'Une révolution conservatrice dans l'édition', *Actes de la recherche en sciences sociales* 126–7 (1999), 3–28.

43 On the role of translation in changes of literary models, see, for example, *Actes de la recherche en sciences sociales* 144 (2002); Johan Heilbron and Gisèle Sapiro, 'Outline for a Sociology of Translation. Current Issues and Future Prospects', in *Constructing a Sociology of Translation,* edited by Michaela Wolf and Alexandra Fukari (Amsterdam: John Benjamins, 2007), 93–107; *Translatio. Le marché de la traduction en France à l'heure de la mondialisation*, edited by Gisèle Sapiro (Paris: CNRS Éditions, 2008); *Les contradictions de la globalisation éditoriale*, edited by Gisèle Sapiro (Paris: Nouveau Monde, 2009); Ioana Popa, *Traduire sous contraintes. Littérature et communisme* (Paris: CNRS Éditions, 2010). On the exchanges between French literature and printing, see Marie-Françoise Melmoux-Montaubin, *L'Écrivain journaliste au XIXᵉ siècle: un mutant des lettres* (Saint-Étienne: Éditions des cahiers intempestifs, 2003) and the following works by Marie-Ève Thérenty: *Mosaïques. Être écrivain entre presse et*

roman (1829–1836) (Paris: Honoré Champion, 2003); *Presses et plumes: journalisme et littérature au XIXᵉ siècle* (Paris: Nouveau Monde, 2004); *La littérature au quotidien, poétiques journalistiques au XIXᵉ siècle* (Paris: Seuil 2007). See also Fanny Bérat-Esquier, 'Les origines journalistiques du poème en prose, ou le siècle de Baudelaire' (doctoral thesis, l'Université Charles de Gaulle, 2006); Pascal Durand, *Mallarmé. Du sens des formes au sens des formalités* (Paris: Seuil, 2008).

44 See Roger Chartier, 'L'écrit sur l'écran. Ordre du discours, ordre des livres et manières de lire', *Entreprises et histoire* 43:2 (2006), 15–25; Dominique Maingueneau, *Contre Saint Proust ou la fin de la littérature* (Paris: Belin, 2006).

45 Pierre Bourdieu, 'Post-scriptum: Du champ national au champ international', in Bourdieu, *Les Structures sociales de l'économie* (Paris: Seuil, 2000), 233–70.

46 Pierre Bourdieu, 'Les conditions sociales de la circulation internationale des idées', *Actes de la recherche en sciences sociales* 145 (2002), 3–8.

47 See Pierre Bourdieu, 'Structuralism and Theory of Sociological Knowledge', *Social Research* 35:4 (1968), 681–706.

48 See Pierre Bourdieu, 'Existe-t-il une littérature belge? Limites d'un champ et frontières politiques', *Études de lettres* 4 (1985), 3–6.

49 See Alain Viala, *Naissance de l'écrivain. Sociologie de la littérature à l'âge classique* (Paris: Minuit, 1985); and, for example, Oliver Christin, 'L'invention de la province artistique', in *L'Espace culturel transnational*, edited by Anna Boschetti, 55–72.

50 Pierre Bourdieu, 'The Market of Symbolic Goods', translated by R. Swyer, *Poetics* 14:1–2 (1985), 13–44. See also Gisèle Sapiro, 'The Literary Field between the State and the Market', *Poetics* 31 (2003), 441–64.

51 Anna Boschetti, *The Intellectual Enterprise. Sartre and 'Les Temps Modernes'*, translated by Richard C. McCleary (Evanston, IL: Northwestern University Press, 1988); and Anna Boschetti, *La Poésie partout. Apollinaire, homme-époque (1898–1918)* (Paris: Seuil, 2001).

52 Pascale Casanova, *The World Republic of Letters*, translated by M. B. DeBevoise (Cambridge, MA: Harvard University Press, 2004).

53 See for example Anna Boschetti, *La Poésie partout. Apollinaire, homme-époque (1898–1918)*; Pascal Durand, *Mallarmé. Du sens des formes au sens des formalités*; Sergio Miceli, 'Jorge Luis Borges, histoire sociale d'un "écrivain-né"', *Actes de la recherche en sciences sociales* 168 (2007), 84–100.

54 See for example Christophe Charle, *Les Intellectuels en Europe au XIXᵉ siècle. Essai d'histoire comparée* (Paris: Seuil, 1996); *Anglo-French Attitudes. Comparisons and Transfers between French and English Intellectuals since the Eighteenth Century*, edited by Christophe Charle, Julien Vincent and Jay Winter (Manchester: Manchester University Press, 2007).

55 Christophe Charle, *La République des universitaires, 1870–1940* (Paris: Seuil, 1994).

56 *Transnational Intellectual Networks. Forms of Academic Knowledge and the Search for Cultural Identities*, edited by Christophe Charle, Jürgen Schriewer and Peter Wagner (Frankfurt: Campus, 2004).

57 Christophe Charle, *Paris fin de siècle. Culture et politique* (Paris: Seuil, 1998).

58 See Christophe Charle, *La Crise littéraire à l'Époque du naturalisme. Roman, théâtre, politique* (Paris: Presses de l'École normale supérieure, 1979) and *Naissance des intellectuels (1880–1900)* (Paris: Minuit, 1990); Gisèle Sapiro, *La Guerre des écrivains, 1940–1953* (Paris: Fayard, 1999); Ioana Popa, *Traduire sous contraintes. Littérature et communisme.*

59 See for example *Capitales culturelles, capitales symboliques. Paris et les expériences européennes*, edited by Christophe Charle and Daniel Roche (Paris: Publications de la Sorbonne, 2002); *Capitales européennes et rayonnement culturel: XVIIIᵉ–XXᵉ siècle,* edited by Christophe Charle (Paris: Éditions Rue d'Ulm/Presses de l'École normale supérieure, 2004); Christophe Charle, *Théâtres en capitales. Naissance de la société du spectacle à Paris, Berlin, Londres et Vienne (1860–1914)* (Paris: Albin Michel, 2008); *Le temps des capitales culturelles (XVIIIᵉ–XXᵉ siècles),* edited by Christophe Charle (Seyssel: Champ Vallon, 2009); Stéphane Van Damme, *Paris, capitale philosophique de la Fronde à la Révolution* (Paris: Odile Jacob, 2005).

60 For instance, French nationalism in the nineteenth century was a response to a European trend coming from Germany. See Anne-Marie Thiesse, 'Une littérature nationale universelle? Reconfigurations de la littérature française au XIXe siècle', in *Intellektuelle Redlichkeit/Intégrité intellectuelle*, edited by M. Einfalt, U. Erzgräber, O. Ette and F. Sick (Heidelberg: Universitätsverlag Winter, 2005), 397–408.

61 See for example Blaise Wilfert, 'Paris, la France et le reste… Importations littéraires et nationalisme culturel en France, 1885–1930' (doctoral thesis, University of Paris I, 2003), and 'L'internationalité d'un nationaliste de Paris: Paul Bourget entre Paris, Londres et Rome' in *L'Espace culturel transnational*, edited by Anna Boschetti, 165–94.

62 See the publications of members of the group ESSE (http://www.espacesse .org/) and CSE (Paris) (http://cse.ehess.fr/). For an overview on the results, methodological suggestions and problems emerging from this collective research, see Christophe Charle, 'Comparaisons et transferts en histoire culturelle de l'Europe. Quelques réflexions à propos des recherches récentes', *Cahiers IRICE* 5 (2009), http://irice.univ–paris1.fr/spip.php?article567.

63 On translation, see the works cited in note 43.

64 On this theoretical exchange between different approaches, see Anna Boschetti, 'Présupposés et vertus de l'échange théorique transnational', *Texte* 45–6 (2009), 153–68.

65 Imre Lakatos, *The Methodology of Scientific Research Programs* (New York: Cambridge University Press, 1978).

Autonomy Revisited: The Question of Mediations and its Methodological Implications

GISÈLE SAPIRO

Abstract:
Bourdieu's concept of the literary field aimed to overcome the opposition between internal and external analysis of literary works. This paper examines its theoretical and methodological implications by exploring the notion of mediations between text and context at three different levels: the material conditions of production and circulation of literary works; the modalities of their production by their authors; their critical reception. It is through these mediations that the key concept of autonomy becomes operational for empirical research and that it displays its heuristic power, as illustrated by works using Bourdieu's theory of the literary field produced over the last two decades.

Keywords: sociology of literature, literary field, autonomy, intellectual history, reception, censorship, Pierre Bourdieu

The question of the autonomy of cultural production is at once an ontological question and a methodological question, these two levels of enquiry being linked.[1] From a methodological standpoint, studies of literary works and other kinds of cultural product can be divided between internal and external approaches. Internal analysis focuses on the act of deciphering rather than on the creative act. The hermeneutical method is based on textual analysis, leaving producers aside. Conversely, external analysis — sociological, historical, or biographical approaches — tends to reduce works to their material conditions of production and reception, ignoring the specificity of symbolic goods. Whereas internal analysis focuses on the structure of works, external analysis insists on their social function.

Paragraph 35.1 (2012): 30–48
DOI: 10.3366/para.2012.0040
© Edinburgh University Press
www.eupjournals.com/para

The question of autonomy was raised by Marxist approaches which replaced the mechanical notion of reflection with the idea of mediation. Lucien Goldmann considered autonomy at the level of works, while Raymond Williams located it at the level of the social conditions of production of literary works.[2] Bourdieu conceptualized it and gave it a sociological application with the concept of field.[3] Contrary to deterministic and mechanical approaches which reduce works and ideas to their material conditions, the concept of field allows us to account for the specificity of cultural or intellectual production and to study the field as a relatively autonomous space. This does not mean that socio-economic constraints do not have any impact on cultural activity, as has been assumed by the ideology of uncreated creators, but that this impact is indirect: it is refracted or mediated through the stakes, the logics of functioning and the structural principles that organize a particular cultural field. Alain Viala has described this as a 'prismatic effect'.[4] Consequently, a sociological analysis of the cultural artefact, considered as a social fact, should include a study of the mediations between works and their social conditions. These mediations can be divided, for analytical purposes, into three groups of phenomena: first, the material conditions of production and circulation of works; second, the modalities of literary production by authors; third, the conditions of the reception of works. These three groups, to be presented here separately, imply three levels of autonomy, which will be examined from both the theoretical and methodological standpoints. Most of the examples are borrowed from literature, but Bourdieu's method of field analysis can also be applied to the history of ideas and the history of art.

The Conditions of Production and Circulation of Works

At the first level, relative autonomy depends on the conditions of production.[5] The two main kinds of external constraint which influence cultural production are ideological and economic: on one hand, the dominant ideology which controls production through state and/or religious institutions, on the other, the market.[6] The means of ideological control vary according to different kinds of regime, but they include control over publication (censorship or restrictions to freedom of speech, lists of prohibited works), trade regulation (in the book or art markets), control over professional organizations and direct repression. To these should be added the system of rewards to intellectuals who serve the interests of the government.[7]

As pointed out by Michel Foucault, the system of control played an important role in the birth of authorship.[8] It also has a direct or indirect impact on cultural production, from explicit orientation (as with socialist realism) to self-censorship.[9] For instance, the manuscripts of Flaubert's *Madame Bovary* reveal the suppression of vulgar expressions such as 'whore' and 'brothel', as well as the suppression of blasphemy and political allusions.[10] These constraints are not limited to legal sanctions, but include good taste, high morals and so forth. Yet censorship and repression can also lead to avoidance strategies, which have often been a source of inventiveness in worlds such as the literary field where agents are used to playing within constraints (verses, the rule of the three unities, etc.). Three major strategies can be identified here: the use of code (allegory, allusion, displacement), publication abroad as a way of skirting national laws and censorship, and illegal activities such as *samizdat*.[11] Avoidance strategies require organization into a chain of production including publishers and printers and a public of initiates able to decipher the message and transmit it along.[12] This is how relatively autonomous literary fields were able to survive even under the authoritarian Vichy and communist regimes.[13]

The conditions of production also define the social role of cultural producers, which is one of the main mediations between works and other external factors. In organized professions, this role is determined by professional bodies. This is why corporatism has often been such a powerful means for controlling cultural production. In return for serving the interests of the State, professionals obtain a monopoly over their activity and are delegated power over their own organizations.[14] Control usually consists of centralizing the means of production, unifying the profession and supervising professional bodies. These means warrant a certain homogeneity of professional recruitment and allow heretical attitudes and activities to be limited or excluded more quickly. Illiberal regimes (absolute monarchy, fascism, or communism) imposed a form of centralized professional organization on cultural activities, which made ideological control of intellectual production easier.[15] Thus, contrary to a common idea in the sociology of professions which considers professional development to imply autonomy, professional organization can in fact be the vehicle for heteronomy.

On the other hand, the repression of cultural activities often brings about a mobilization of cultural producers in defence of autonomy. Since the sixteenth century, scientists have grounded their quest for truth on reason and experience, to combat religious dogmatism. It was on the basis of these values that the intellectual field affirmed its autonomy with regard to the religious field in the eighteenth century.[16] The literary and artistic fields declared their autonomy from the field of ideological production by separating the 'beautiful' and the 'useful', a distinction based on Kant's theory of disinterested aesthetic judgement. While Romanticism promoted the ideal of beauty, Realism appropriated the value of objectivity from the scientific field, which was gaining authority at the time. To represent reality in an objective and 'true' way became an artistic value, aimed at protecting cultural production from ethical judgement. Realist writers like Flaubert, Descaves and Zola brandished these values against the accusations they faced of offending high morals. In this sense, the struggle against political control contributed to the forging of the principles and values upon which the relative autonomy of the intellectual field is based.[17] This is why in illiberal regimes the defence of autonomy is often associated with political struggle, to which it is however subordinate within the field. In fascist and communist regimes, to tell the truth in the midst of lies became the professional ideology of dissidence among such authors as Bertolt Brecht in Germany or Paul Goma in Romania.

Whereas the claim to autonomy from the religious field favoured the emergence of an intellectual field grouped around common values such as truth, disinterestedness, reason and critical judgement,[18] the nineteenth century was marked by the 'division of expert labour'.[19] This involved the differentiation of a space of activity through the emergence of a body of specialists, its institutionalization and the exclusion of the uninitiated (laymen or 'amateurs'), a phenomenon described by Max Weber in the case of religion and law. This process of monopolization can be more or less successful, depending on various factors: the conditions of access (academic training, diplomas, competition or entrance examination), which can be more or less stringent; the homogeneity of the professional group according to its social recruitment and to the conditions of practice; competition, internal or external (with other professions); the strength of monopoly over the activity (jurisdiction); the level of official recognition of professional bodies and their power to impose their rules on the body of specialists.[20]

Though professional development can be observed in the literary field from the mid-eighteenth century, with the rise of literary societies and demands for the recognition of authors' rights,[21] writers never became a 'profession' in the Anglo-American sense. Moreover, the division of intellectual work and expert labour had consequences for the literary field, as it had for the religious field. The resulting dispossession in certain domains such as morality, politics and knowledge provoked counter-reactions, which developed into two significant postures: either withdrawal to the ivory tower and art for art's sake (which can be considered as the equivalent of mysticism in religion), or alternatively engagement, the latter split between conservative and even reactionary stances based on alliances against science and democracy at the heteronomous pole, and at the autonomous pole the commitment of the public intellectual embodied by Emile Zola during the Dreyfus Affair.[22]

Support for the differentiation of intellectual activities can often be found in the division of powers. In seventeenth-century France, a new category of symbolic producer appeared: writers who distinguished themselves from academics by using the French vernacular rather than Latin, and who promoted culture for entertainment rather than erudition. These authors were sustained by the absolute Monarchy, which aimed to unify the kingdom at the linguistic level, and which in return for their services delegated to writers the power to legislate on linguistic matters (the *Académie française* was given an official status in 1635). Autonomy from the religious field thus implied submission to the government.[23] While the development of the book market constituted a counter-power which allowed intellectual producers progressively to escape State control and patronage, the liberalization of the circulation of printed matter as well as the industrialization of book production in the nineteenth century led to a high dependency of cultural producers on the demand of the public, and so introduced a new principle of heteronomy. New genres such as the serial novel (published in newspapers) allowed some writers, including Eugène Sue, to adjust to this demand, and to modify their projects in light of the opinions of their readers — transmitted, for instance, through their letters.[24] This is why, as Bourdieu showed, Flaubert and others affirmed the autonomy of literature from the market in the second half of the nineteenth century, by claiming the superiority of the judgement of their peers and other specialists over those of the uninitiated public. This claim implied a distinction between the aesthetic value of the work and its commercial value — a distinction that is still challenged by the market. Investigating the recent evolutions of the publishing field, in what happened to be his last empirical inquiry,

Bourdieu demonstrated the increasing weight of economic constraints on the book market, including concentration and the growing influence of financial capital, which tend to exclude the most autonomous products or genres, such as poetry or experimental writing.[25]

The higher the degree of autonomy, the less direct impact external constraints have on works. Their influence appears in the works, but in a distorted way, as if refracted by a prism, and it is sometimes difficult to recognize. In relatively autonomous spaces, external constraints are refracted through more or less institutionalized bodies: training institutions (academic training, specialized schools), social spaces (literary circles, learned societies), instances of consecration (prizes, academies, salons), professional bodies (associations, trade unions). The fact these bodies exist is evidence of a certain degree of autonomy within the field in question, but they can also be vehicles for heteronomy in the field. The case of the French literary field under the German Occupation provides an example of the way literary institutions which had in the past played a major role in the processes of autonomization can become instruments for the imposition of ideological constraints on literature.[26] The majority of members of the *Académie française* supported the Vichy regime; the *Académie Goncourt* awarded its prestigious prize to a regionalist writer, Henri Pourrat, who was celebrated by the regime as embodying the policy of return to the land; the *Nouvelle Revue française*, which had been a proponent of pure literature in the interwar period, became, after excluding Jewish and anti-nazi writers, a showcase for Franco-German collaboration. The failure of these institutions to defend the autonomy of the literary field led writers in the opposition to organize and in some cases join the intellectual Resistance, the infrastructure of which was in large part managed by the Communist Party. This is how the *Comité national des écrivains* (National Committee of Writers) was born, an underground organization which became an association after the Liberation. But again, autonomy was recovered thanks to an external counter-power, the Communist Party, which introduced another new principle of heteronomy.

Whereas the notion of profession implies unity and homogeneity, the concept of field allows us to grasp the principles that structure relatively autonomous spaces of cultural activity, and which represent another mediation between political and economic constraints and works themselves. The opposition between those who occupy dominant and dominated positions is one such principle, and crosses all fields.[27] It often opposes 'established' writers and 'newcomers' in the field, but it can also be based on social differences, such as, in the eighteenth century, between writers endowed with official functions and literary bohemia.[28] During the same period, an opposition also appeared between 'organic intellectuals', in Antonio Gramsci's terms, and intellectuals who claimed their autonomy from political and religious powers on the basis of their charismatic authority and reputation among the public. This opposition between heteronomy and autonomy is a second principle structuring fields of cultural production. These principles define a relational space of positions which is homologous, according to field theory, to the space of position-takings. This last point leads us to look at the second level of autonomy.

Modalities of Production of Works: The Producer's Viewpoint

Sociological analysis of the production of works requires, according to Bourdieu's theory, a study of the relation between a habitus and a field, understood as a *space of possibilities*. The conception of field as a space of possibilities stems from the relational approach, which displaced essentialist hermeneutics in the history of ideas (Cassirer, Foucault), the history of art (Panofsky) and literary history (the Russian formalists, Even-Zohar's polysystem theory). In the history of ideas, this developed as *Geistesgeschichte*, following Ernst Cassirer, who elaborated a neo-Kantian approach to the study of symbolic forms. Bourdieu, who was a reader and translator of Cassirer from 1960, was especially influenced by his book *Substance and Function*, which looked to replace essentialism with functionalism.[29] In 1963, Bourdieu devoted his seminar at the École normale supérieure to the history of art (Haskell, Riegl, Wölfflin, Panofsky, etc.), and translated into French Erwin Panofsky's *Gothic Architecture and Scholasticism*, which uses a relational approach.[30] In the postface to this translation, Bourdieu proposed his first analysis of the concept of habitus. In literary history, the conception of a structured and historical space of thematic, stylistic and linguistic possibilities can be traced back to the Russian formalists, whose systemic approach was developed by Even-Zohar with the concepts of 'polysystem', a structured and hierarchized system of texts, and that of a 'repertoire' of models (themes, styles, linguistic options) available at a given moment.[31] Whereas French structuralism was a-historical, in 1968 Foucault proposed an historical approach using the notion of 'episteme', defined as a 'field of strategic possibilities' but limited to the field of discourses. In their seminal article on the 'primitive forms of classification', Durkheim and Mauss also paved the way for a socio-historical analysis of categories of perception.[32]

Whereas the hermeneutic approach focuses on structures as they are perceived by *lectores*, that is professional readers or commentators — works being thought of as individual expressions of a universal structure, as the 'parole' was for Saussure — Bourdieu was interested from the outset in the *modus operandi*.[33] He was engaged in research on the sociology of action, with a focus on agents, which led him in 1972 to publish *Outline of a Theory of Practice*.[34] Though he criticized it as overly rational, he adopted Sartre's notion of a creative project.[35] In Sartre's ultra-individualist and subjectivist perspective, the creative project seems to be a conscious strategy, present from the start and anchored in the biography of the individual subject, as illustrated by Sartre's biography of Flaubert.[36] Bourdieu stressed the pre-reflexive aspects of practice and introduced the mediation of the field as a space of possibilities.

How does the individual agent internalize the space of possibilities, and how does her or his presence modify this space? This is a crucial question, and one of the conditions for field reflexivity (reference to its own history), which is itself one of the main characteristics of autonomy. The answer is far from obvious, when we come to put field theory into practice. Firstly, because the space of possibilities appears differently according to an agent's habitus and the position (s)he occupies in the field. The space of positions which constitute a given configuration of the field is objectively structured by the unequal distribution of the different kinds of capital: one can speak of a 'space of biographical possibilities'.[37] It is a space of viewpoints that founds the homology between the space of positions and the space of position-takings. We must therefore ask in addition: how does a particular cultural producer perceive the space of positions and the space of possibilities at any given moment? In relation to which positions does she or he define himself? What options does this space offer the writer, given the kinds of capital with which (s)he is endowed? These are questions with no a priori answer, but which should guide our research at the methodological level.

To sum up, we need to study the mediations between the space of intellectual possibilities and the space of biographical possibilities. These mediations are partly institutional. A major institutional mediation is the school. General education is part of what founds the principle of self-referentiality in spaces of cultural production such as the literary field which do not have a specialized training of their own, by instilling common reference points and manners of thinking. In this respect, education offers an interesting basis for the comparison of national intellectual fields and for analysis of the conditions of exchange between them.[38] Humanist culture has shaped the Western intellectual habitus since the sixteenth century. In France in the nineteenth century, only children of the bourgeoisie had access to high school, where humanism was taught. Humanism began to be challenged by scientific culture at the beginning of the twentieth century and has been declining since the 1960s. The surrealists belong to the first generation of French writers who did not share a humanist education. This predisposed them to subvert a tradition of which they were not the heirs.[39]

School is not the only mediation operational in a social world such as literature, access to which often depends on demonstrations of autonomy and distance towards the educational system, because of the old rivalry between writers and professors, *auctores* and *lectores*.[40] The notions of 'fashion' or 'news' are a good expression of these 'social trends', as Durkheim called them,[41] which impose at each moment the order of priorities, the 'agenda', the dominant taste, what was once called the *Zeitgeist*. In the intellectual field, publications set the rhythm of these trends: newspapers, specialized reviews, reprints, new publications, translations. For example, the reprints of Cervantes's *Don Quixote* in the nineteenth century and translations of Goethe and Byron were determining factors in the genesis of Flaubert's literary project, as the translations of Faulkner, Hemingway and Dos Passos were for that of Sartre. In his study on Heidegger, Bourdieu demonstrates that the *völkisch* mood, which was dominant during the Weimar Republic, impregnated the philosopher's work, but was transformed by the categories of philosophical thought to such an extent that it became unrecognizable.[42] This transformation illustrates the field effect, that is to say the way the available literary models or philosophical concepts reshape common representations. One way for an intellectual to distinguish himself from the culture of the school is to (re)discover unknown writers, as the surrealists did with Lautréamont, or to refer to products of popular culture, as the surrealists again did with *Fantômas* by Marcel Allain and Pierre Souvestre. But even when we have, as we do for Flaubert or Sartre, reliable sources documenting their readings, the traces of which can be found in their works — such as the implicit references to Shakespeare or Cervantes in Flaubert — this does not suffice to account for the transubstantiation performed by the creative act, which remains a 'black box'.

The representation of material borrowed from experience, imagination, fashion or history cannot be separated from literary models and the work on style, from the putting into form. Both aspects, representation and formalization, are linked to the author's viewpoint and therefore to his habitus, but formalization is the most specific process whereby the field effect, and so autonomy, can be detected. It is noteworthy, in this respect, that the law on authorship protects only form and not content. The space of possibilities is not internalized in complete isolation. Reactions, feedback and sanctions, before and after publication, orient the choices of newcomers and lead them to readjust their strategies. Flaubert's friends Bouilhet and Du Camp, after he read to them his *The Temptation of Saint Anthony* a whole night through, told him to throw it away. From this event arose the project to write *Madame Bovary* — as a way to counterbalance his romantic dispositions, his friends suggested that he should choose a more common and contemporary subject, in the tradition of Balzac's *Cousin Pons* or *Cousine Bette*.[43]

In contradistinction to the impersonal bureaucratic world, the lower the level of institutionalization in a field, the greater is the role played by interactions and personal relations. Nevertheless, relational analysis of the structure of a space cannot be reduced to interactions.[44] The space of positions is a relational space that is objectively structured, as mentioned, according to the distribution of social properties. For example, in the French literary field of the nineteenth century, the psychological novelists had higher social origins and more scholastic capital than the naturalists (some of them studied psychology at university).[45] Along the same lines, structural analysis of the space of works, considered as a relational system, is at odds with essentialist hermeneutics. As in structural linguistics, the meaning of works is defined by the system of differential gaps. The system of oppositions gives meaning to the positions taken. For instance, the writers of the *Nouveau Roman* were connected less by a shared set of themes and devices than by a similar rejection of the main elements of composition in the realistic novel: social identification of characters, plot and message.[46] Their reference to Flaubert and the theory of 'art for art's sake' should also be understood in terms of its opposition to Sartre's conception of committed literature, which dominated the French intellectual field of the 1950s.

Far from leading to a sociological reductionism which would dissolve the original nature of works in the 'social', it is only by taking such an approach that we can understand the real originality of a work.

Bourdieu's concept of a 'symbolic revolution' designates the process by which innovative works redefine the space of possibilities. This redefinition, which modifies the principles of perception and practices, is an objective fact, which can often be measured by the scandal these works provoke when they are first presented to the public: for instance, Flaubert's use of 'free indirect speech' paved the way for the modern novel. Contrary to their peers who reproduce models more than they create new ones, these cultural producers transform the space of possibilities, as has been illustrated by works on Beckett by Pascale Casanova or on Apollinaire by Anna Boschetti.[47] But such innovations are not produced *ex nihilo*. As Thomas Kuhn showed in the case of scientific revolutions,[48] they often derive from the importation of models and devices from another field, or from the synthesis between apparently opposite options: for example, Flaubert imported devices from painting and the theatre into the novel; he also flouted the classical separation between beautiful style and socially 'low' subjects (the milieu of the provincial *petite bourgeoisie*).

Reception

The meaning of a text cannot be reduced to the intention of its author. Any work, like any action, has a meaning that is independent from the will of the author, stemming from its very position in the space of possibilities and in the real space of symbolic productions, which is objectively structured, as well as from its various interpretations and annexations. For example, during the German Occupation in France, to publish or not to publish had a political meaning independent from writers' intentions. A critic of both positivist literary history and the Marxist theory of reflection on the one side and of a-historical hermeneutics on the other, Hans-Robert Jauss has suggested an anti-positivist literary history based on reception, considered as the history of the effect that works produce. The key concept is that of *Erwartungshorizont* (the horizon of expectations), borrowed from Husserl, Mannheim and Popper. As Jauss argues, the trial of *Madame Bovary* demonstrates that a new aesthetic device can have moral consequences.[49] The principle of impersonal narration was such a new device which, in association with free indirect speech, led the prosecutor to commit an error of interpretation, and to confuse the author for the character.[50]

Trials are interesting for the study of reception because they reveal the limits of what can be expressed or represented in a given socio-historical configuration.[51] During trials, the interpretation of the work is at stake. But there are other cases of discussion concerning the interpretation of works that are quite interesting for the study of the reception process, illustrating as they do not only rejection but also annexation. For instance, *Voyage au bout de la nuit* (*Journey to the End of the Night*) by Céline was praised by right-wing as well as by left-wing critics. His lampoon *Bagatelles pour un massacre* (*Trifles for a Massacre*) provoked a debate between the Catholic philosopher Jacques Maritain and the writer André Gide: while Maritain denounced Céline's anti-Semitism, Gide argued that Jews were a metaphor. Gide tried, in this way, to maintain Céline's association with the autonomous subfield, even though his choice of the genre of lampoon, as well as his use of extreme-right newspapers as sources, indicated Céline's evolution towards increasing heteronomy.[52]

According to Jauss, the horizon of expectations can be based on internal analysis of works. But like production, reception is a process which is mediated. The material and intellectual presentation of works, the comments made by specialists, the way they are appropriated by different kinds of readership according to their social properties, all these aspects of reception were pointed out by the founders of 'Cultural Studies', Richard Hoggart and Raymond Williams, and their programme was developed in the sociology of culture and the history of art, literature and ideas.[53] For written works, the paratext (preface, postscript), the medium (newspaper, specialized magazine, book), the surroundings (in a newspaper or in a series), are all elements which condition the process of reception. A preface can, for instance, orient the interpretation of a work independently of the author's intent, as when Sartre annexed Nathalie Sarraute's 1948 *Portrait d'un inconnu* (*Portrait of a Man Unknown*) to existentialist literature.

Since Bourdieu's pioneering research on museum-goers and Hoggart's study on the reading of popular novels,[54] a great deal of research has been done on reception by the public, from modalities of appropriating works to studies of readers' trajectories.[55] I shall focus here on critical reviews, which are a major source for reception studies and which are more directly connected to the question of autonomy. This source has often been exploited by historians of art, literature and ideas, since it corresponds well to the interpretative tradition of their disciplines.[56]

The positive or negative sanctions that a work receives can contribute to the redefinintion of the space of possibilities. This was for example the case with Sartre's famous review of *La Fin de la nuit* (*The End of the Night*) by the established Catholic writer François Mauriac. Sartre denounced his use of the device of the omniscient narrator. Such a viewpoint was impossible according to Einstein's theory of relativity, he argued. Mauriac, he said, had conflated the narrator's position with that of God: 'God is not a novelist. Nor is Mr Mauriac.'[57] This review had an effect not only on Mauriac's trajectory (he wrote his next novel, *La Pharisienne* (1941, *A Woman of the Pharisees*), using the first person and then stopped writing novels for a long time), but also on the whole field, where it contributed to the devaluation of the device of the omniscient narrator. Reception conditions in turn the trajectory of an author, who sees him- or herself in the image that is sent back to him and in the expectations of the public, to which he or she has to adapt. The case of Romain Gary, who had to adopt a pseudonym in order to be able to change his style (and in the process obtained the Goncourt prize for a second time under the name of Émile Ajar), reveals *a contrario* the weight of these expectations.

Criticism implies selection, evaluation and hierarchization, which are crucial to the question of autonomy. Field effects can be located in the selection and classification performed by critics and newspapers, through the diffusion of works and in the process of their hierarchization, consecration and canonization: sales, recognition by peers or critics, literary prizes, institutional consecration, political annexations are indicators of these complex procedures. Different kinds of success can be contradictory: for example, in France since the middle of the nineteenth century, sales and literary recognition are not only distinguished but even opposed. Selling a large number of copies of a book is often considered as a sign that the author has adjusted himself to the demand of the public, in other words as a mark of heteronomy.

According to the positions they occupy, agents' criteria for judging a work vary. We can thus propose a model for analysing critical discourse, derived from the structure of the field. The discourse on art and literature varies according to two main factors. The first, which opposes the 'dominant' to the 'dominated', distinguishes orthodox from heterodox approaches. In effect, the more dominant an agent's position is, the more she or he tends to adopt a formal, euphemistic and depoliticized discourse, according to the 'etiquette' of

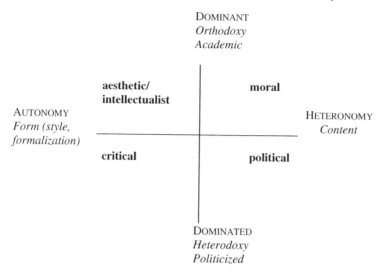

Figure 1. Ideal types of critical discourse.

academic debate. Conversely, the more an agent occupies a dominated position, the more (s)he tends to denounce in academicism a kind of conformism, and to adopt a politicized discourse. The second factor is organized around the opposition between autonomy and heteronomy. According to this opposition, critical discourses on art and literature focus either on content (theme, story, plot, moral values) or on formal and stylistic aspects (narration, poetics, composition). This second tendency illustrates the principle of autonomy in that it expresses the autonomy of aesthetic judgement with regards to morality, together with the increasing reflexivity of the field of cultural production, as demonstrated by the reference to its own history.

By cross-classifying these two factors — dominant/dominated and autonomy/heteronomy — we obtain four ideal types of discourse on art and literature (figure 1). Moral judgement prevails at the dominant heteronomous pole, while social or political criteria are most representative of the dominated discourse at this pole. At the pole of autonomy, aesthetic judgement characterizes the dominant positions, while the avant-gardes see art and literature as a means of political subversion.

Conclusion

The autonomy of cultural fields is only relative, since heteronomous forces are involved in the process of cultural production. At the methodological level, this implies that a real study of cultural production requires a cross-disciplinary approach combining both external analysis and internal reading, while taking into account the mediations between these two orders of phenomena. The educational system, the definition of the social role of the producer, professional ideology, the structure of the field, the space of possibilities and the reception process are all major mediations, without this list being exhaustive.

The degree of autonomy of cultural production in a socio-historical situation is an empirical question, which can be studied at the three levels of mediation described in this paper. The first is the social conditions of production. Once autonomy from religion is acquired, equilibrium between State regulation and the market can ensure a relative degree of autonomy for cultural producers. Whereas historically the aspiration for freedom of trade sustained the fight for freedom of speech, these days the State counterbalances the market logic which reduces literary and artistic works to commercial goods. Yet autonomy also depends on the social practices of cultural producers. One of the findings of this approach is that professionalization was not a necessary condition for the autonomy of cultural production. Conversely, certain forms of politicization which lay emphasis on the critical function of intellectual activity have been consubstantial with the conquest of autonomy. The dispositions for disinterestedness common to cultural producers who engage in cultural production and circulation as a vocation (not for profit), according to their own specific values, are the main social condition for autonomy. At the second level, an indicator of autonomy at the level of works is their degree of formalization, which involves a reference to the history of the field. The third level is that of reception. The existence of an aesthetic judgement, free from moral or political considerations, as well as from economic expectations, is an indicator of a high degree of autonomy.

Finally, it should be remembered that for Bourdieu autonomy was not only a theoretical and methodological question, but also a normative one: autonomy is the condition for freedom of creation and literary innovation. Having gained a relative autonomy from the State and from religion, the question writers and other cultural producers confront today is how to maintain a degree of autonomy in a global system which is more than ever ruled by the law of the market, and which tends to exclude non-commercial genres such as poetry or experimental writing.

NOTES

1   A previous version of this paper was presented at the conference 'Practicing Pierre Bourdieu: In the Field and across the Disciplines' at the University of Michigan, 28–30 September 2006.

2   Lucien Goldmann, *The Hidden God: A Study of Tragic Vision in the Pensées of Pascal and the Tragedies of Racine* [1955], translated by Philip Thody (London: Routledge, 1964) and 'Critique et dogmatisme dans la création littéraire', in Lucien Goldmann, *Marxisme et sciences humaines* (Paris: Gallimard, 1970), 41; Raymond Williams, *Marxism and Literature* (New York: Oxford University Press, 1977), 95–100.

3   Pierre Bourdieu, 'The Field of Cultural Production, or: The Economic World Reversed', *Poetics* 12:4–5 (1983), 311–56; 'Le champ littéraire', *Actes de la recherche en sciences sociales* 89 (1991), 4–46; *The Rules of Art: Genesis and Structure of the Literary Field* [1992], translated by Susan Emanuel (Cambridge: Polity Press, 1996); *The Field of Cultural Production. Essays on Art and Literature*, edited by Randal Johnson (Cambridge: Polity Press, 1993).

4   Alain Viala, 'Prismatic Effects', *Critical Inquiry* 14:3 (1988), 563–73.

5   Pierre Bourdieu, 'Le marché des biens symboliques', *L'Année sociologique* 22 (1971), 49–126.

6   Gisèle Sapiro, 'The Literary Field between the State and the Market', *Poetics* 31:5–6 (2003), 441–61.

7   Jérôme Karabel, 'Towards a Theory of Intellectuals and Politics', *Theory and Society* 25 (1996), 205–23.

8   Michel Foucault, 'Qu'est-ce qu'un auteur?' [1969], *Dits et Écrits I: 1954–1988* (Paris: Gallimard, 1994), 789–820.

9   Régine Robin, *Le Réalisme socialiste. Une esthétique impossible* (Paris: Payot, 1986).

10 Claudine Gothot-Mersch, *La Genèse de Madame Bovary* (Paris: Corti, 1966), 246–8.

11 Gisèle Sapiro, 'The Literary Field between the State and the Market'.

12 Robert Darnton, *The Literary Underground of the Old Regime* (Cambridge, MA: Harvard University Press, 1982).

13 Roger Chartier, *The Cultural Origins of the French Revolution*, translated by Lydia Cochrane (Durham, NC: Duke University Press, 1990); Gisèle Sapiro, *La Guerre des écrivains (1940–1953)* (Paris: Fayard, 1999), English translation forthcoming from Duke University Press; Ioana Popa, *Traduire sous contraintes. Littérature et communisme (1947–1989)* (Paris: CNRS Editions, 2010).

14 Magali Sarfatti-Larson, *The Rise of Professionalism: A Sociological Analysis* (Berkeley/Los Angeles/London: University of California Press, 1977); Jan Goldstein, '"Moral Contagion": A Professional Ideology of Medicine and Psychiatry in Eighteenth- and Nineteenth-Century France', in *Professions*

   and the French State: 1700–1900, edited by Gerald. L. Geison (Philadelphia: University of Pennsylvania Press, 1994), 181–222.

15 On the Unions of Russian and Romanian writers, see for example Johan and Caroll Garrad, *Inside the Soviet Writers' Union* (New York/London: The Free Press/Macmillan, 1990); Lucia Dragomir, *L'Union des écrivains. Une institution transnationale à l'Est* (Paris: Belin, 2005).

16 Didier Masseau, *L'Invention de l'intellectuel dans l'Europe du XVIIIe siècle* (Paris: PUF, 1994).

17 Gisèle Sapiro, *La Responsabilité de l'écrivain. Littérature, droit et morale en France (XIXe–XXIe siècle)* (Paris: Seuil, 2011).

18 Christophe Charle, *Naissance des 'intellectuels' 1880–1900* (Paris: Minuit, 1990).

19 Andrew Abbott, *The System of Professions. An Essay on the Division of Expert Labor* (Chicago and London: The University of Chicago Press, 1988); Christophe Charle, *Les Intellectuels en Europe au XIXe siècle. Essai d'histoire comparée* (Paris: Seuil, 1996).

20 Gisèle Sapiro, 'Les professions intellectuelles, entre l'État, l'entrepreneuriat et l'industrie', *Le Mouvement social* 214 (2006), 3–24.

21 Gisèle Sapiro and Boris Gobille, 'Propriétaires ou travailleurs intellectuels? Les écrivains français en quête de statut', *Le Mouvement social* 214 (2006), 119–45.

22 Christophe Charle, *Naissance des 'intellectuels' 1880–1900*; Gisèle Sapiro, 'Forms of Politicization in the French Literary Field', *Theory and Society* 32 (2003), 633–52; Gisèle Sapiro, 'Défense et illustration de "l'honnête homme": les hommes de lettres contre la sociologie', *Actes de la recherche en sciences sociales* 153 (2004), 11–27; Hervé Serry, *Naissance de l'intellectuel catholique* (Paris: La Découverte, 2004).

23 Alain Viala, *Naissance de l'écrivain. Sociologie de la littérature à l'âge classique* (Paris: Minuit, 1985); Christian Jouhaud, *Les Pouvoirs de la littérature. Histoire d'un paradoxe* (Paris: Gallimard, 2000).

24 Anne-Marie Thiesse, 'L'éducation sociale d'un romancier: le cas d'Eugène Sue', *Actes de la recherche en sciences sociales* 32–3 (1980), 51–64.

25 Pierre Bourdieu, 'A Conservative Revolution in Publishing' [1999], translated by Mieranda Vlot and Anthony Pym, *Translation Studies* 1:2 (2008), 123–54. See also John B. Thompson, *Merchants of Culture. The Publishing Business in the Twenty-First Century* (Cambridge: Polity Press, 2010).

26 Gisèle Sapiro, *La Guerre des écrivains (1940–1953)*.

27 Pierre Bourdieu, 'Some Properties of Fields', in Bourdieu, *Sociology in Question* [1984], translated by Richard Nice (London: Sage, 1993), 72–7.

28 Darnton, *The Literary Underground of the Old Regime*.

29 See Ernst Cassirer, *Substance and Function* [1910], translated by W. C. Swabey and M. C. Swabey (New York: Dover, 1953); a French translation was

published in a collection edited by Bourdieu as *Substance et fonction*, translated by Pierre Caussat (Paris: Minuit, 1977).

30 Erwin Panofsky, *Architecture gothique et pensée scolastique*, translated with postface by Pierre Bourdieu (Paris: Minuit, 1967).

31 Itamar Even-Zohar, 'Polysystem Studies', *Poetics Today* 11:1 (1990) (special single-authored issue).

32 Émile Durkheim and Marcel Mauss, 'De quelques formes primitives de classification' [1903], in Marcel Mauss, *Œuvres*, Vol. 2 (Paris: Minuit, 1974), 13–89.

33 Pierre Bourdieu, 'Pour une science des œuvres', in *Raisons pratiques. Sur la théorie de l'action* (Paris: Seuil. 1994), 59–98.

34 Pierre Bourdieu, *Outline of a Theory of Practice* [1972], translated by Richard Nice (Cambridge: Cambridge University Press, 1977).

35 Pierre Bourdieu, 'Champ intellectuel et projet créateur', *Les Temps modernes* 246 (1966), 865–906.

36 Jean-Paul Sartre, *The Family Idiot: Gustave Flaubert, 1821–1857* [1971–2], translated by Carol Cosman, 5 vols (Chicago: University of Chicago Press, 1981).

37 Christophe Charle, *La République des universitaires, 1870–1940* (Paris: Seuil, 1994).

38 Fritz Ringer, *Fields of Knowledge. French Academic Culture in Comparative Perspective, 1890–1920* (Cambridge: Cambridge University Press, 1992).

39 Norbert Bandier, *Sociologie du surréalisme. 1924–1929* (Paris: La Dispute, 1999).

40 Anna Boschetti, *The Intellectual Enterprise: Sartre and 'Les Temps Modernes'* [1985], translated by Richard C. McCleary (Chicago: Northwestern University Press, 1988).

41 Emile Durkheim, *The Rules of Sociological Method* [1895], translated by W. D. Halls (London: Macmillan, 1982).

42 Pierre Bourdieu, *The Political Ontology of Martin Heidegger* [1988], translated by Peter Collier (Cambridge: Polity, 1991).

43 Maxime Du Camp, *Souvenirs littéraires*, 2 vols (Paris: Hachette, 1883), I, 405–42.

44 Gisèle Sapiro, 'Réseaux, institutions et champ', in *Les Réseaux littéraires*, edited by Daphné de Marneff and Benoît Denis (Bruxelles: LE CRI/CIEL-ULB-Ug, 2006), 44–59.

45 Remy Ponton, 'Naissance du roman psychologique: capital culturel, capital social et stratégie littéraire à la fin du 19e siècle', *Actes de la recherche en sciences sociales* 4 (1975), 66–81.

46 Alain Robbe-Grillet, *Pour un nouveau roman* (Paris: Minuit, 1963).

47   See Pascale Casanova, *Beckett. Anatomy of a Literary Revolution*, translated by Gregory Elliott (London/New York: Verso Books, 2007); Anna Boschetti, *La Poésie partout. Apollinaire, homme–époque (1898–1918)* (Paris: Seuil, 2001).

48   T. S. Kuhn, *The Structure of Scientific Revolutions* [1962] (Chicago: University of Chicago Press, 1996).

49   See Hans Robert Jauss, 'Literary History as a Challenge to Literary Theory', in Jauss, *Toward an Aesthetic of Reception*, translated by Timothy Bahti (Minneapolis: University of Minnesota Press, 1982), 3–45.

50   Dominick LaCapra, *'Madame Bovary' on Trial* (Ithaca: Cornell University Press, 1982).

51   Sapiro, *La Responsabilité de l'écrivain*.

52   Alice Kaplan, *Relevé des sources et citations dans 'Bagatelles pour un massacre'* (Tusson: du Lérot, 1987).

53   Richard Hoggart, *The Uses of Literacy* [1970], with a new introduction by Andrew Goodwin (New Brunswick, NJ: Transaction Publishers, 1992); Raymond Williams, *Culture* (London: Fontana Press, 1981).

54   Pierre Bourdieu and Alain Darbel, *The Love of Art: European Art Museums and their Public* [1969], translated by C. Beattie and N. Merriman (Cambridge: Polity, 1990); Hoggart, *The Uses of Literacy*.

55   Anne-Marie Thiesse, *Le Roman du quotidien. Lecteurs et lectures populaires à la Belle Epoque* (Paris: Le Chemin vert, 1984); James Smith Allen, *In the Public Eye: a History of Reading in Modern France, 1800–1940* (Princeton, NJ: Princeton University Press, 1991); Claude Fossé-Poliak, Gérard Mauger and Bernard Pudal, *Histoire de lecteurs* (Paris: Nathan, 1999).

56   See for example Joseph Jurt, *La Réception de la littérature par la critique journalistique: lectures de Bernanos, 1926–1936* (Paris: J.-M. Place, 1980).

57   Jean-Paul Sartre, 'M. François Mauriac et la liberté' [1939], *Critiques littéraires (Situations I)* (Paris: Gallimard, 1993), 53.

The Literary Field and the Field of Power: The Case of Modern China

MICHEL HOCKX

Abstract:

This article discusses ways in which Pierre Bourdieu's literary sociology has inspired scholarship on modern Chinese literature, helping it to move away from overly politicized paradigms of literary historiography. The article also asks the question to what extent the use of a Bourdieusian model has resulted in an overemphasis on the 'relative autonomy' of a literary field that, at various times during the twentieth century, has been operating under conditions of strong direct state interference. After giving a general overview of the use of Bourdieu's ideas in the study of modern Chinese literature, the article focuses especially on the question of autonomy and the state, arguing for the study of state censors as specific 'agents' within the literary field. The article ends with a brief discussion of the rapid rise of online literary communities in China, their practices and their relation to state institutions.

Keywords: Pierre Bourdieu, China, literary field, field of power, socialism, censorship, internet literature

Introduction

In my only ever direct communication with the late Pierre Bourdieu, via email in 1996, he expressed surprise that his ideas about literature could be applied to such an 'alien' field as the study of Chinese literature. Sure enough, for scholars who have debated the use of Bourdieu's field model in understanding literary production in non-Western societies, the question of 'applicability' has often loomed large.[1] It is not always clear, however, to what extent those sceptical of Bourdieu's framework are genuinely concerned about its cross-cultural

Paragraph 35.1 (2011): 49–65
DOI: 10.3366/para.2012.0041
© Edinburgh University Press
www.eupjournals.com/para

potential and to what extent their critique is based on a general distaste for the sociological method. Consider, for instance, the comment cited below, from a scholar of modern Chinese literature expressing reservations about Bourdieu's approach:

Bourdieu's theory provides an interesting dimension through which to consider the emergence of revolutionary literature, involving an analysis of the historical development of the available possibilities in literature within the broader field of power on the one hand and an account of the individual and class habitus that engenders strategies of competition on the other. However, *Bourdieu's Francocentric observation of the literary field that is based on cultural capital or symbolic capital cannot fully explain the utopian desire, the nationalist implication, the semicolonial sentiment, or an individual's sensuous and bodily experience that are implicated in the movement of 'revolutionary literature'.* Besides leftists' competition for the hegemonic discourse of revolution in the literary field, they were also practically involved in the libidinally charged revolutionary waves.[2]

In the passage I have underlined, the suggestion that 'Francocentrism' is to blame for a lack of understanding of revolutionary sentiment comes across as paradoxical. After all, France has stood at the cradle of all modern revolutionary movements. The real objection expressed here is about genuinely experienced desires and sentiments as well as genuine commitment to a political cause being 'reduced' to strategic elements in the struggle for symbolic capital. Other scholars of modern Chinese literature have expressed similar concerns without referencing Francocentrism or Eurocentrism. Haiyan Lee's investigation into the 'literary public sphere' of early twentieth-century China dismisses Bourdieu's model in a footnote. The underlined passage, culminating in a rhetorical question, essentially reiterates the objection noted above:

[R]ecasting the literary public sphere as a 'cultural field' or subfield in which (. . .) writers, publishers, editors, and readers produced, circulated, and consumed cultural products while competing with other agents (. . .) for control of material and symbolic capital would no doubt yield many insights. *However, I remain unconvinced by the theoretical purchase of Bourdieu's 'general science of the economy of practices', armed as it is with metaphors of interest, investment, capital, profit, and the like, on transformations of value, identity, and solidarity. Can the economic logic of maximizing material and symbolic profit exhaust the range of actions and goals that agents pursue in the cultural field?*[3]

The most succinct expression of the same objection can be found in Mabel Lee's review of the Bourdieu-inspired collection *The Literary*

Field of Twentieth-Century China.[4] Lee writes: 'Some individuals have a commitment to art, literature, scholarship or some other cultural activity as a vocation and embrace that calling in a way which falls outside the slide-rule ratio proposed by Bourdieu for symbolic capital and economic capital.'[5]

The emphasis in these cited passages on the significance of human actions and emotions beyond strategic profit maximization is clearly indebted to what Bourdieu would have called the *doxa* of literary and cultural studies in the Western academy, and indeed of the literary field. 'Reducing' literary production to an essentially economic activity (albeit in a 'reversed economy') goes against widely held beliefs and is therefore to be resisted. I do not think that Bourdieu ever set out to deny the complexity of human agency nor the strength of human beings' convictions regarding their personal and professional commitments. On the contrary, I think Bourdieu took these things extremely seriously (hence his emphasis on studying the concept of habitus) but at the same time he would have insisted that the objective existence of long-standing structures and relatively stable positions ensures that much human agency is in fact predictable and can very well be reduced to a smaller number of principles. This understanding is crucial to the distinction between 'positions' and 'position-takings': the economic reality of being in the position of 'literature professor' requires the habitual taking of positions about literature that downplay or deny its economic characteristics.

Nevertheless, the fact that scholars of modern Chinese literature are interacting with Bourdieu's ideas, even if they do not always agree with them, is evidence of his impact and standing in a field that he thought of as 'alien'. Below are a few comments on the general positioning of modern Chinese literature in wider scholarly and critical communities. After that I shall turn to a discussion of ways in which Bourdieu's ideas have enriched specific studies by anglophone and sinophone scholars.

The Global Positioning of Modern Chinese Literature

There is, of course, an even more compelling reason why scholars of modern Chinese literature, especially those working outside China, prefer to emphasize the complexity and autonomy of literary creation. That is the fact that, for much of the modern period, Chinese literary production (including criticism and scholarship of literature) took place in the context of a socialist system. The basic positions in the anglophone study of modern Chinese literature took shape during the Cold War.[6] Left-wing Western and Eastern European scholars emphasized the historical relationship between modern Chinese literary production, the Communist revolution and the processes of decolonization and nation-building.[7] Their opponents engaged in exploration of the aesthetic excellence of some pre-1949 (pre-Communist) work as well as work from post-1949 Taiwan, and in exposing the oppression of artistic autonomy under Communist rule.[8] Both sides of the divide represented strong opinions on the relationship between literature and politics, while they were united in their dismissal of market-driven literary production.

Much has changed since then, but scholarly and writerly position-takings in relation to the socialist system or Communist rule continue to play an important role in the assignment of literary or intellectual value to Chinese-language work, although it is fair to say that the enthusiasm for the Communist experiment among left-wing anglophone scholars has waned considerably. Chinese writers who express outspoken sympathy for the Communist regime now generally lack critical reception in the anglophone scholarly community, whereas those who express outspoken opposition have a better chance of being taken seriously. This is true all the more when it comes to the positioning of modern Chinese literary works in the global publishing market and the field of non-academic criticism. Generally speaking it benefits Chinese writers, when dealing with Western critical contexts, to emphasize their autonomy from not one but two heteronomous principles, namely 'politics' and 'the market'. This principle is best illustrated by a statement from Gao Xingjian, winner of the Nobel Prize for literature in 2000. When asked what the award signified to him, Gao responded: 'With this prize it is recognized that I write neither to make money nor to serve a political power.'[9] The suggestion that winning a prize of roughly one million pounds has nothing to do with making money is wonderfully paradoxical, yet undoubtedly entirely sincere, and perfectly in line with Bourdieu's observations.[10]

Bourdieu would perhaps have been more surprised that Gao felt the need to emphasize that he does not 'serve a political power', since this is a gesture that few Western writers consider it necessary to make.[11] But in the 'alien' context of the modern Chinese literary field, political capital plays an important role. In my own three-dimensional adaptation of Bourdieu's schematic representation of the literary field, I suggest that successful trajectories inside the modern Chinese literary field involve a careful balancing act between striving for critical recognition (symbolic capital), for political efficacy without sacrificing independence (political capital) and for discreet money-making (economic capital).[12]

The political efficacy sought by many modern Chinese writers revolves mainly around domestic issues. That is why, as early as 1971, the critic C.T. Hsia coined the pejorative phrase 'obsession with China' to describe what he considered to be a 'parochial' lack of 'universal value' inherent in modern Chinese fiction.[13] Three decades later, Pascale Casanova put forward a similar argument by stating that Chinese writers had 'long found themselves shut off from the literary world in a state of quasi-autarky'.[14] The term 'quasi-autarky' is well-chosen, since it reflects well the self-perception of the Chinese socialist literary system prior to the 1980s. Moreover, the carefully formulated phrase 'found themselves shut off' reflects the fact that modern Chinese writers did not all choose to be sidelined from participation in the global literary world. At the same time, Casanova's account of some Chinese writers' responses to the award of the Nobel Prize to Gao Xingjian highlights the kind of 'nationalist' sentiments that she sees as obstructive to the accumulation of the main currency in the world republic of letters: 'universality' (147–8).

There can be no doubt that 'politics' plays a significant role in modern Chinese literary production. However, the emphasis on politics as the dominant category to explain or critique the activities of twentieth-century Chinese authors has been waning for some time now. For most anglophone scholars of modern Chinese literature who have positively interacted with Bourdieu's ideas, including myself, the main attraction of his approach has been that it allowed us to grasp the political element in relational terms and to highlight how symbolic and economic principles are at work throughout the modern period.

Bourdieu-inspired Anglophone Studies of Modern Chinese Literature

Most narratives of the development of modern Chinese literature postulate a 'mainstream' of politically engaged leftist literature that gradually grew in importance from the late 1910s onwards and eventually emerged victorious at the same time as the Communist revolution. Needless to say this narrative is itself greatly indebted to *post facto* Communist historiography. When the Chinese socialist system began to reform itself in the 1980s and access to library collections was once again possible for non-Chinese scholars, many chose to focus on studying material that did not belong to, or was at odds with, the supposed 'mainstream'. Moreover, those scholars choosing to study contemporary Chinese literary developments also focused almost exclusively on so-called 'non-official' (*fei guanfang*) literature, meaning literature not supported by the state system, or on the 1980s avant-garde, which was considered to pose a challenge to the official system (more about this below). Much attention was also paid to more commercial types of literary production, to continuities between the premodern tradition and modern writing, and to the specificities of (post)colonial power relations and gender relations at work in cultural production. A wide range of theorists provided inspiration for that work. Those who chose to follow a Bourdieusian approach were encouraged by his ideas to emphasize the relative autonomy (in this case from politics) of the literary field, as well as the various position-takings that occurred outside the mainstream.

As far as I know, the first book-length study of modern Chinese literature to make meaningful reference to Bourdieu's ideas about literature is Xiaomei Chen's *Occidentalism*, published in 1995. In her discussion of 1980s Chinese drama, Chen mentions Bourdieu when discussing the strategic use of 'occidentalism' and claims of western 'influence' by members of a theatrical avant-garde keen to establish a position for themselves within the literary field.[15] Very substantial reference to Bourdieu can be found in Ravni Thakur's 1997 monograph *Rewriting Gender*, which explores gender discourses and the strategic use of the concept of 'women's literature' by writers and critics in 1980s China. Thakur explicitly hails the concept of the 'literary field' as a useful tool to modify overly generalist analyses of gender discourse.[16] My 1999 edited collection *The Literary Field of Twentieth-Century China* contains Bourdieu-inspired essays by various scholars dealing with such previously non-mainstream topics as the role of translation, the genre of love-letter writing, the publishing practices of contemporary popular fiction, and the lifestyle of avant-garde poets. My 2003 study of Chinese literary societies and literary magazines of the 1920s and 1930s argues for recognizing a variety of competing 'styles' at work within a high-speed literary economy with no single mainstream.[17] John Christopher Hamm's 2005 monograph on the hugely popular Hong Kong martial arts writer Jin Yong references Bourdieu extensively, especially in its analysis of the complex process by which Jin, and the genre he represents, rose to canonical status and scholarly recognition.[18]

Bourdieu's ideas also strongly influenced Sung-sheng Yvonne Chang's comprehensive study of the literary culture of modern Taiwan, published in 2004.[19] Although Taiwanese literature lies outside the scope of this article, Chang's study is worth mentioning for two reasons. Firstly, in her ambition to map out the entire modern literary field of Taiwan, including both state-supported and independent writing, she comes closer than any of the scholars mentioned above in attempting the kind of analysis that Bourdieu put forward for modern France. Secondly, in identifying her work emphatically as a form of 'contextual study', Chang has articulated most clearly the attraction that Bourdieu holds for many scholars of literature: as a move away from and a reaction to the still very dominant text-based, 'intrinsic' approach to literary studies. I think it is fair to say that, although Bourdieu himself insisted on having transcended the opposition between 'intrinsic' and 'extrinsic' approaches, the 'intrinsic' side of his work, namely his close readings of fiction by Flaubert and Faulkner, is not what has attracted most of his followers. What attracts most people to his ideas is his sophisticated analysis of how literary communities operate and relate to other parts of society. This is also clear when we look at Bourdieu's impact on literary scholarship in China itself.

Bourdieu in China

According to the China Academic Journals (CAJ) database, the first introduction to Bourdieu in the Chinese mainland appeared in the journal *Quanqiu jiaoyu zhanwang* (Survey of Global Education) in 1979. The article in question is a Chinese translation of David Swartz's 'Pierre Bourdieu: The Cultural Transmission of Social Inequality', originally published in the *Harvard Educational Review* in 1977. Interest in Bourdieu's ideas developed slowly over the course of the 1980s, with only a handful of occurrences of his name in academic articles in the fields of education and sociology. Although some of these articles mention that Bourdieu also has an interest in the study of literature, Chinese scholars did not seem to take an interest in his work in this area until the mid-1990s. In 1993, the book review journal *Dushu*, hugely popular among intellectuals for its brief, up-to-date introductions to Western theory, published an article on Bourdieu's concept of 'symbolic capital' by the literature scholar Wang Ning;[20] in 1995, the same journal published an article explaining the term 'cultural capital';[21] in 1996 it published my Chinese-language summary of Bourdieu's sociology of literature, as grasped from my reading of *The Field of Cultural Production* and the Dutch translation of *The Rules of Art*.[22] It seems that these publications were part of a wider trend, with Chinese interest in all aspects of Bourdieu's work sharply increasing in the mid-1990s and gradually overtaking interest in the work of other major French theorists of the same generation.[23]

Bourdieu's reputation among Chinese scholars of literature was further cemented with the publication of the Chinese translation of *The Rules of Art*, by Liu Hui, in 2001.[24] As far as I know, the main impact of his work on Chinese scholars of modern Chinese literature has been similar to what was noted above about the anglophone community.[25] Bourdieu's model of the literary field and the interaction of capital, habitus and position is employed most enthusiastically in 'contextual' studies aiming to present a broader overview of literary production of any given period, or to rehabilitate previously ignored or marginalized authors, works and trends. As such, Bourdieu-inspired work has contributed to the drive towards 'rewriting literary history', which started in the 1980s and which aimed at debunking the overly politicized narrative of Chinese twentieth-century literary history, especially with regard to the pre-1949 period. If previous historiography focused on the rise of the leftist movement throughout the 1920s and 1930s, current scholarship now goes into great descriptive detail about the commercial system of literary production that was established in cities like Shanghai from the late nineteenth century onwards.[26] Bourdieu's ideas have also inspired critical reflection on the past, present and future of the Chinese socialist literary system, raising questions about the relationship between the literary field and the field of power, to which I now turn.

The Socialist System

The Chinese socialist literary system, established in Communist-controlled areas of China during the War of Resistance against Japan (1937–45) and the Civil War that followed it (1945–9), was implemented on a nationwide scale after the founding of the People's Republic in October 1949. As pointed out by Perry Link,[27] the Chinese system was initially largely modelled on the Soviet system: literary production was planned and controlled by national and regional propaganda departments and by party committees inside publishing houses, as well as by an overarching state organization known as the All-China Federation of Literary and Artistic Circles, one of whose subsidiaries was the Writers' Association. The Writers' Association arranged the editorial boards of literary magazines, provided stipends to amateur writers and employed a small elite of full-time professional writers (118–22). Prior to the Cultural Revolution (1966–76), writers were well-paid: they received fees for manuscripts as well as royalties based on the number of copies of their work that was printed. The decision on how many copies to print was often a planning decision, made by the bureaucracy, and never solely a commercial decision based on demand (130).[28] During the Cultural Revolution, the Writers' Association ceased to function and all payments to writers were stopped (131). Although recent scholarship has argued that Cultural Revolution China was not the kind of cultural wasteland it has been considered to be,[29] it is difficult to detect any significant measure of autonomy nor any obvious symbolic distinction mechanisms for literary producers of the period, at least not in the public sphere.

The doxa of socialist literary production (in China, and presumably also in the Soviet bloc) is well captured in the following lines from Link's study:

> To understand how socialist China's literary control system worked, the Western observer must first set aside deeply ingrained notions about the primacy of the writer. In the design of the system, the primary relationship, which all the other relationships were supposed to support, was that between top leadership and readers. The purpose of literature was to lead readers to think what the leadership determined it was best that they think. (65)

The 'control' mentioned here was achieved through a system of censorship described by Link as follows:

> Socialist China did not have the kind of formal censorial organs that other autocratic regimes have maintained. Literary control was less mechanical, and more psychological, than it has been elsewhere. It depended primarily on the private calculation of risks and balances in the minds of writers, editors, and those who supported them. (81)

When the socialist system was gradually phased out in the 1980s and replaced by a market-driven system under state control, this meant that the primary function of literature was no longer propaganda. Psychological control of writers, however, remained in place, albeit in an ever more relaxed form. As a result, the 'private calculation' of political risks was more and more often balanced by calculations of potential economic and symbolic gains. This is what, in my view, makes the postsocialist literary field more complex than any of the fields described by Bourdieu.

The Inclined Literary Field

A very original critique of the contemporary Chinese literary field, heavily inspired by Bourdieu, has been put forward by Peking University professor Shao Yanjun in her 2003 monograph *The Inclined Literary Field*, and in several articles published since then.[30] In the course of her studies and during her previous career in the publishing industry, Shao gathered impressive amounts of empirical information dealing especially with Chinese literary institutions of the 1980s. There is an existing image of the 1980s as an era of tremendously exciting intellectual fermentation, especially in the arts and humanities, and feverish interest in new, experimental forms of artistic expression. The 'obscure poetry' and 'avant-garde fiction' of the 1980s is generally credited with having overthrown the previous socialist realist paradigm and (re)instated the values of 'pure literature' in China. Shao makes very fruitful use of Bourdieu in pointing out how 'pure literature' was promoted by a small elite, behaving very much like the 'producers producing for other producers' that Bourdieu described so well. Moreover, Shao argues, in the 1980s the socialist system had not yet been completely dismantled and this new literary elite not only reaped symbolic profits but also profited from continued state support for writing, publication and distribution. Shao writes:

Writers were showing off to editors, editors were showing off to critics, critics were showing off at conferences, and behind it all was the magazine publication system supported by the Writers' Association, and the university system. Inevitably, this developed towards cliquishness — and these cliques were not communities of individuals with similar tastes, but interest communities of individuals sharing the same privileges. (...) From the postal system that allowed the free sending of manuscripts for submission, to the patronage of and generous instruction to writers by the editors of the big magazines; from the formal establishment of culture bureaus at prefecture level to the assistance with revising manuscripts, free travel and lodgings provided by the big magazines, the whole emergence and development of the avant-garde movement relied on the latent continuity of the traditional literary mechanism.[31]

Towards the end of the 1980s, the Chinese government started 'weaning' the literary system off state support. By that time, according to Shao, the 'pure literature' trend and its 'cliques' had alienated so many readers that many literary magazines and publishing houses ran into trouble. As a result, the field of serious literary production started to incline more and more towards the field of market-driven popular literature. This 'inclined literary field' works against any attempts by producers of serious literature to develop truly autonomous literary institutions.

Shao's unexpected solution to the problem of the inclined literary field is to argue for a return to left-wing realism — the discarded 'mainstream' of modern Chinese literature (21). Her statistics show that throughout the 1980s and 1990s, authors of socially engaged realist fiction, despite being maligned by the cliquish critical establishment, were able to command significant readerships. Moreover, their works continued to be read by large numbers of people over a long period of time, making them different from market-driven 'bestsellers', which are typically quickly forgotten once the hype has passed. In short, Shao Yanjun's Bourdieu-inspired analysis of the contemporary Chinese literary field ends in a paradox that somehow makes perfect sense: the pure literary field of the 1980s and all its seemingly autonomous literary values was in fact a state-sponsored system; and in order to obtain more autonomy from the state, and from the market, the Chinese literary field should adopt a version of the ruling party's ideology. This would allow it to gather sufficient followers (readers) to break off any latent reliance on state support, while at the same time resisting market pressure.

The Literary Field and the Field of Power

Bourdieu situated the literary field inside the field of power, at the lower end of the power scale. Although in other parts of his work he had plenty to say about politics and the power of the state, I think it is fair to say that his thinking about the literary field occupied itself more with autonomy vis-à-vis the power of the market. He viewed the literary world as 'the economic world reversed' and symbolic capital, at least as it operates in the cultural field, as the opposite of economic capital. Although he mentions political authorities and even censorship in the context of the 'structural subordination' of cultural producers to the dominant class,[32] mediated through the market and through state patronage, he presents no specific study of censorship. And although he brilliantly analyses Zhdanovism in terms of 'resentment' (281) and in terms of heteronomy arriving in a field 'through the producers who are the least capable of succeeding according to the norms it imposes' (347), he does not study in detail the position occupied by state bureaucrats in the literary field, nor the relation of such a position to other positions.[33]

Bourdieu's work has had a stimulating impact on the study of modern Chinese literature by calling attention to ways in which literary communities can be relatively autonomous and by broadening our perspective beyond the Cold War political dualism and beyond the politicized narrative of 'mainstream' development. Yet the emphasis on autonomy and the introduction of more and more different authors, group and styles should not detract from the fact that, throughout virtually the entire modern period, the Chinese literary field was operating under conditions of state interference and state control. The links between state-supported and field-generated literary institutions and practices can be quite complex and are perfectly well analysable with Bourdieusian tools. The practices of censors, for instance, are worth taking seriously. Censors are literary producers in their own right. They contribute to the making of the text, often through negotiations and power exchanges with writers, editors and publishers, as I have shown in the case of literary censorship in Shanghai in the 1930s.[34] In the Communist period, and even nowadays, censors and editors have often been one and the same person. As Shao Yanjun's research shows, even during what was considered the most 'autonomous' period of literary production in contemporary China, the powerful position of editors, as both beneficiaries of state privileges and cultivators of young writers in search of symbolic capital, is well worth studying.

Finally, let us return to Shao's suggestion that an autonomous (i.e. non-state-supported) form of left-wing writing could keep the Chinese literary field from inclining too much towards vulgar market mechanisms. The underlying idea here (and, I would argue, a key element of the habitus of many involved in literary production in modern China) is that good literature deserves a large readership, because literature has something important to contribute to the nation. And writers must attempt to stay in constant touch with that readership, by publishing frequently and addressing the most pressing concerns of their era. One aspect of Bourdieu's reversed economy never gained ground in modern China: whether one looks at the 1920s or at the 1990s, the idea that spending more time on producing a single literary work can lead to greater recognition (symbolic capital) is alien to the modern Chinese writer. Virtually all modern Chinese writers write fast and publish much. Distinction is achieved through frequent interaction with the readership.

This is one of the many reasons why the current 'boom' in web literature in China is so fascinating. From the late 1990s onwards, Chinese Internet users have been remarkably enthusiastic about using online discussion forums (also known as BBS) to publish and discuss literary work. Web literature is a term that is part of most educated people's vocabulary, and recent developments in the world of web writing are discussed at length in newspapers, while the most successful web-based works also appear in print. Many writers of high literature, including some that were involved in the 1980s avant-garde, have turned to web writing to continue their formal and linguistic experiments. But popular genre fiction has also moved online and can be found on hugely popular internet portals where readers can purchase subscriptions that allow them to follow the serialization of new works chapter by chapter and to leave comments on each chapter for the author to read and respond to, often resulting in plots changing halfway through a work in response to readers' comments. For all practical purposes, these websites act as publishers but, crucially, they are not state-owned, whereas all print publishers in China still are. This suggests a new form of autonomy in the making.

Web literature has produced celebrities, such as the essayist cum racing driver Han Han, as well as serious writers with very loyal online followers, such as the novelist Anni Baobei (literally 'Annie Baby'). Both have recently converted their online fame by crossing over into the world of print publishing and making attempts to launch independent literary magazines with no ties to state offices. Websites also produce their own 'webzines' as well as online anthologies. They organize competitions for literary prizes, but web writers are by now also regularly considered for the country's most highly regarded state-sponsored literary prizes.

As is well known, the Internet in China is also censored, but because this censoring is largely done by machines looking for specific keywords rather than by actual people reading texts, the control can be easily circumvented and has in fact given rise to all kinds of linguistic innovations, such as deliberate misspellings of sensitive words, writing such words in transliteration or in English, or inserting an asterisk between two characters so that they no longer appear as a single word. As far as literature is concerned, the Internet is changing the rules of the game in China. The outcome is uncertain, but the balance of power between state, market and cultural producers is definitely shifting and new tastes, new sub-fields and new distinction mechanisms appear to be opening up. More widely, the Chinese Internet is also a contested space. Large businesses attempt to exploit it to make money, the state attempts to control it in order to cling to power, cultural producers attempt to create their own niches on it to further their autonomy, while Western observers, often harking back to the old Cold War stereotypes, attempt to turn it into a token of 'freedom' that is cruelly suppressed by a Communist government. The complex forces at work in this new 'field' are unquestionably suited to the kind of relational analysis that Bourdieu pioneered, and that it is up to us to expand and improve.

NOTES

1 For a general discussion of charges of 'Eurocentrism' against Bourdieu's sociology of literature, see my 'Theory as Practice: Modern Chinese Literature and Bourdieu', in *Reading East Asian Writing: The Limits of Literary Theory*, edited by Michel Hockx and Ivo Smits (London and New York: RoutledgeCurzon, 2003), 220–5.

2 Jianmei Liu, *Revolution Plus Love: Literary History, Women's Bodies, and Thematic Repetition in Twentieth-Century Chinese Fiction* (Honolulu: University of Hawai'i Press, 2003), 36; emphasis added.

3 Haiyan Lee, 'All the Feelings That Are Fit to Print: The Community of Sentiment and the Literary Public Sphere in China, 1900–1918', *Modern China* 27:3 (2001), 291–327 (323); emphasis added.

4 *The Literary Field of Twentieth-Century China*, edited by Michel Hockx (Honolulu: University of Hawai'i Press, 1999). A set of conference papers that were later to result in this collection was sent by me to Pierre Bourdieu in late 1995, which led to his short email message to me in January 1996.

5 Mabel Lee, *The China Journal* 44 (2000), 160–2 (161).

6 English is by far the most important language for the global study of Chinese literature. Publication in English yields considerably more academic capital than publication in other Western languages. Nevertheless, there are active communities for the study of modern Chinese literature in countries such as Germany and France, and their paradigms have at times developed differently from those of anglophone scholars.

7 The most important proponent of this position (and the most vocal assailant of the opposite position) was Professor Jaroslav Prušek from Charles University, Prague, whose 1960s writings on the subject were endorsed by many in the Western academy, to the extent that a canonical North American collection of essays on early modern Chinese literature, published in 1977, was dedicated to his efforts. See *Modern Chinese Literature in the May Fourth Era*, edited by Merle Goldman (Cambridge, MA: Harvard University Press, 1977).

8 Special mention should be made here of the brothers T. A. Hsia and C. T. Hsia, whose widely read English-language monographs criticizing Communist suppression of literature and celebrating the literary excellence of individual non-Communist writers epitomize this important founding position in the anglophone field of modern Chinese literary studies. See Tsi-an Hsia, *The Gate of Darkness: Studies on the Leftist Literary Movement in China* (Seattle: University of Washington Press, 1968) and C. T. Hsia, *A History of Modern Chinese Fiction* (New Haven: Yale University Press, 1961; second revised edition, New Haven and London: Yale University Press, 1971; third edition, Bloomington and Indianapolis: Indiana University Press, 1999).

9 ' "Das Absurde ist die Form unserer Existenz" ' ('The Absurd is the Shape of Our Existence'), *Welt Online*, 14 October 2011, http://www.welt.de/print-welt/article538421/Das_Absurde_ist_die_Form_unserer_Existenz.html, consulted 22 March 2011, 5.12 p.m.

10 I should add that the anglophone community of modern Chinese literature scholars has in fact been rather dismissive of Gao Xingjian's achievement. He has found much more support especially among francophone scholars and critics, not entirely surprisingly since he lives in France and has French nationality. The fact that the first Chinese Nobel laureate has such a strong 'French connection' lends support to Pascale Casanova's Bourdieu-inspired hypothesis that views Paris as the centre of the global literary field. See Casanova, *The World Republic of Letters*, translated by M. B. DeBevoise (Cambridge, MA: Harvard University Press, 2004).

11 Note, however, that the Nobel committee itself made similar gestures. The scholar Julia Lovell, inspired by Bourdieu, argues that the basic stance of the post-World-War-II committee in awarding the literature prize comes down to a double rupture: 'We detest those who write for money, but we detest just as much those who write for politics.' Lovell, *The Politics of Cultural Capital: China's Quest for the Nobel Prize in Literature* (Honolulu: University of Hawai'i Press, 2006), 61.

12 Michel Hockx, 'Introduction', in *The Literary Field of Twentieth-Century China*, edited by Hockx, 1–20 (17).

13 Hsia, *A History of Modern Chinese Fiction*, third edition, 533–54.

14 Casanova, *The World Republic of Letters*, 147.

15 Xiaomei Chen, *Occidentalism: A Theory of Counter-Discourse in Post-Mao China* (New York and Oxford: Oxford University Press, 1995). Note that in the revised and expanded second edition of this book (Lanham, MD: Rowman & Littlefield, 2002), the argument remains in place and Bourdieusian terms such as 'cultural capital' are still used, but the only specific reference to Bourdieu in the main text was removed and his works no longer appear in the bibliography. This may simply have been an oversight or it may signal that terms such as 'cultural capital' have now become commonplace and no longer require direct references to Bourdieu.

16 Ravni Thakur, *Rewriting Gender: Reading Contemporary Chinese Women* (London: Zed Books, 1997).

17 Hockx, *Questions of Style: Literary Societies and Literary Journals in Modern China, 1911–1937* (Leiden: Brill, 2003).

18 John Christopher Hamm, *Paper Swordsmen: Jin Yong and the Modern Chinese Martial Arts Novel* (Honolulu: University of Hawai'i Press, 2005).

19 Sung-sheng Yvonne Chang, *Literary Culture in Taiwan: Martial Law to Market Law* (New York: Columbia University Press, 2004).

20 Wang Ning, 'Xiangzhengxing ziben yu xiangzhengxing baoli' (Symbolic Capital and Symbolic Violence), *Dushu* 1993:5, 104–9.

21 Chen Yangu, 'Wenhua ziben' (Cultural Capital), *Dushu* 1995:6, 134–6.

22 He Maixiao (Michel Hockx), 'Budi'e de wenxue shehuixue sixiang' (Bourdieu's Thoughts on the Sociology of Literature), *Dushu* 1996:11, 76–82.

23 The relatively strong interest in Bourdieu in China, in comparison to the anglophone world, can be most strikingly visualized by using the Google Ngram tool to map references to 'Bourdieu, Derrida, Foucault' for the period 1980–2008 in the Google English corpus and the Simplified Chinese corpus. Simplified Chinese is the script used in Mainland China, as opposed to Traditional Chinese which is used in Taiwan and Hong Kong. Although the Google Ngram is an experimental tool, this distinction should ensure that the corpus searched consists largely of texts produced in Mainland China.

24 Piaier Budi'e (Pierre Bourdieu), *Yishu de faze* (*The Rules of Art*), translated by Liu Hui (Beijing: Zhongyang bianyi chubanshe, 2001).

25 Undoubtedly Bourdieu has had an influence on Chinese scholars of non-Chinese literature as well, perhaps especially on the sinophone study of French literature, but I am not familiar with any of that work.

26 A recent example is Li Jiping's study of the establishment of the modern institutions of literary publishing, distribution and criticism in the 1920s. See Li, *Wenxue yanjiuhui yu Zhongguo xiandai wenxue zhidu* (The Literary Association and the Modern Chinese Literary System) (Beijing: Zhongguo chuanmei daxue chubanshe, 2010).

27 Perry Link, *The Uses of Literature: Life in the Socialist Chinese Literary System* (Princeton: Princeton University Press, 2000). Link's book does not reference Bourdieu but its detailed description of the workings of the system, emphasizing comparisons with the Soviet situation as well as with Western market-driven systems, makes it an extremely useful reference in this context. There is also a recent Chinese-language study of the system, which does reference Bourdieu and goes into great detail in documenting the various relevant institutions. See Wang Benchao, *Zhongguo dangdai wenxue zhidu yanjiu (1949–1976)* (Approach to Institutions of Chinese Contemporary Literature [1949–1976]) (Beijing: New Star Press, 2007).

28 As Link points out (131), the greatest financial beneficiary of the system was Mao Zedong himself, as he received huge amounts of royalties for his mass-produced political writings.

29 See for instance Paul Clark, *The Chinese Cultural Revolution: A History* (New York: Cambridge University Press, 2008).

30 Shao Yanjun, *Qingxie de wenxuechang: dangdai wenxue shengchan jizhi de shichanghua zhuanxing* (The Inclined Literary Field: The Commercial Transformation of Contemporary Literary Production Mechanisms) (Nanjing: Jiangsu renmin chubanshe, 2003). For an English-language discussion of Shao's work, see also Marco Fumian, 'The Temple and the Market: Controversial Positions in the Literary Field with Chinese Characteristics', *Modern Chinese Literature and Culture* 21:2 (2009), 126–66.

31 Shao Yanjun, 'Chuantong wenxue shengchan jizhi de weiji he xinxing jizhi de shengcheng' (The Crisis of the Traditional Literary Production Mechanism and the Rise of a New-Style Mechanism), *Wenyi zhengming* 12 (2009), 12–22 (13–14).

32 Pierre Bourdieu, *The Rules of Art: Genesis and Structure of the Literary Field*, translated by Susan Emanuel (Stanford: Stanford University Press, 1996), 49–50.

33 In his essay on censorship in *Language and Symbolic Power*, Bourdieu also shows a much greater interest in censorship as internalized 'forms of perception and expression' than in concrete negotiations and interactions between cultural producers and representatives of the State. See Bourdieu, *Language and Symbolic Power*, translated by Matthew Adamson, edited by John B. Thomson (Cambridge: Polity Press, 1991), 138.

34 Hockx, *Questions of Style*, 222–51.

Between Repression and Anamnesis: Pierre Bourdieu and the Vicissitudes of Literary Form

Jeremy F. Lane

Abstract:

Pierre Bourdieu's work on literature has frequently been criticized for its perceived failure to attend to the specificities of literary form. This article argues that, in fact, literary form plays an important role in Bourdieu's theorizations of literature, or rather, that form is called upon to play a range of different, potentially conflicting roles. Through close readings of both *The Rules of Art* and the 1975 essay 'L'Invention de la vie d'artiste' (The Invention of the Life of the Artist), the article seeks to clarify the different roles Bourdieu attributes to literary form, as that which both conceals and reveals 'repressed', 'incorporated' or 'unconscious' social realities. It will examine Bourdieu's contention that the literary work functions analogously to the Freudian dreamwork in this respect, and will question how appropriate or convincing that analogy proves to be.

Keywords: Pierre Bourdieu, literary form, anamnesis, repression, socioanalysis, psychoanalysis, Flaubert, *Sentimental Education*

In an article of 1991, Toril Moi concluded that, whatever Pierre Bourdieu's work might have to offer feminist theory, its value to feminist literary studies was strictly limited, since, 'insofar as his is not a theory of textuality at all, a purely Bourdieusian reading' of literary texts would be 'unthinkable'.[1] Two years later, Jacques Leenhardt seemed to confirm Moi's contention that Bourdieu's sociology of literature was unable to account for the specificities of the literary form and of the kinds of truth to which it might offer access. He argued that Bourdieu's analyses of literary texts were marked by a questionable dichotomy between sociological reason and literary form, the former

Paragraph 35.1 (2012): 66–82
DOI: 10.3366/para.2012.0042
© Edinburgh University Press
www.eupjournals.com/para

corresponding to the domain of objective, scientific truth, the latter relegated to the realm of the sensual, the magical, of embodied belief and repressed truth, against which sociology defined itself.[2] Morag Shiach has also criticized what she sees as the failure by Bourdieu to take any account of literature's specific characteristics. In a critique of the reading Bourdieu offers of Virginia Woolf's *To the Lighthouse* in his analyses of 'masculine domination', Shiach regrets his tendency 'to treat the novel as a series of descriptions rather than as a text that might embody contradiction or offer a formal challenge to the categorial differences [between the sexes] with which it begins'.[3]

On the basis of this admittedly incomplete survey of critical responses, it would appear that a consensus has emerged to the effect that, whatever his sociology of culture may have to offer the study of literature, Bourdieu's work has little of value to say about the specificities of textuality or literary form. This article will argue that whilst this critical consensus is not wholly without justification, it can only be maintained at the cost of underestimating the extent of Bourdieu's engagement with the specificities of literary form. That said, a closer reading of Bourdieu's various analyses of literary form will not uncover a wholly consistent theory capable of refuting all of the criticisms levelled by Moi, Leenhardt, and Shiach. Rather, it will reveal literary form to occupy a paradoxical space within Bourdieu's sociology of literature, presented alternately as that instance which ensures the repression of the truths contained in literature and as the very force which reveals those truths through 'anamnesis'.

At first glance, the contention that Bourdieu's sociology of culture might have difficulties acknowledging the specific or inherent value of literary or indeed of artistic form would seem broadly justified. Inasmuch as it is accorded a specific role at all in Bourdieu's work, literary form appears to feature above all as the means whereby such sociological truths as may be contained within narrative fiction are concealed or 'euphemized'. This process of concealment and 'euphemization' is seen as being a necessary precondition for any sociological truth either to be articulated within a pre-existing field of literary production or to be received in its homologous field of reception. Were those truths to be expressed in their unvarnished or un-euphemized form, Bourdieu argues, they would not qualify and hence would not be received as literature at all. Bourdieu develops these ideas on literary form in the course of the successive interpretations he offers of Flaubert's 1869 novel *Sentimental Education*, interpretations published in a series of articles from the mid-1970s onwards, which in turn fed into the book-length study *The Rules of Art* (1992). At the core of these interpretations is Bourdieu's claim that Flaubert's novel contains a peculiarly accurate depiction, and 'an extraordinarily successful (and quasi-scientific) objectification', of the relationships between political power, the economy and the artistic field in mid-nineteenth-century France.[4] Frédéric Moreau, the novel's young protagonist, negotiates these different worlds, hesitating and ultimately failing to commit himself to pursuing a career in any of them. The condition of possibility of such hesitancy is the family fortune Frédéric stands to inherit, an inheritance which means he is under no immediate compulsion to commit himself to a career and is able to look with some disdain at the compromises necessarily involved in making any such career commitment.

If Flaubert is able to objectify so accurately the different social fields through which Frédéric moves, this is because, Bourdieu argues, of the similarities of social origin, class habitus and social trajectory between the novelist and his fictional character. As a young man, Flaubert too benefited from an inheritance which disposed him to look disdainfully on the various career positions open to him. As an adult novelist, this inheritance is the condition of possibility of Flaubert's 'double refusal' of the two primary possibilities the contemporary state of the literary field offered him, in the form of the immediate financial rewards of 'l'art bourgeois' (bourgeois art) or the political engagement implicit in 'l'art social' (social art). Through his refusal of those two positions and of the temporal rewards they offer, and with the financial support of his inherited wealth, Flaubert can thus occupy a 'neutral place'; 'that *neutral place* where one can soar above groups and their conflicts, the struggles waged by different kinds of intellectuals and artists among each other, and those which pit them against all the different varieties of "property owners"' (*RoA*, 26). Through the narrative of his fictional character Frédéric, then, Flaubert undertakes 'an enterprise of *objectification* of the self, of autoanalysis, of socioanalysis'. However, Flaubert remains distinct from his hesitant protagonist, as from his hesitant younger self, through the very act of writing, an act which distinguishes him from the 'indetermination' and 'impotence' of the fictional Frédéric. Hence writing *Sentimental Education* becomes an act by which Flaubert 'sublimates' his younger self, Gustave, 'through the retrospective appropriation of himself that he secures by writing the story of Frédéric' (*RoA*, 25). Through retrospectively appropriating the dispositions, assumptions and behaviour, in short the habitus and trajectory of his younger self, Flaubert manages to objectify both the determinants and motivations of someone of his social class and the coordinates of the social fields through which such an individual might have charted a path.

At this stage of Bourdieu's reading of *Sentimental Education* it would seem difficult to distinguish Flaubert's fictional account of nineteenth-century French society from a sociological account of that same society; each would appear to offer equal access to the truth or objectivity of that social world. It is at this point in his analysis that Bourdieu turns to the specific role of literary form, arguing that it functions to euphemize and conceal the sociological truths that the literary text nonetheless reveals. Thus he turns to Flaubert's notebooks, maintaining that these contain in brute, unvarnished form a version of the novelist's 'expressive intention', prior to its being euphemized by being put into literary form. As he puts it in *The Rules of Art*, in 'the notebooks in which Flaubert outlined the plots of his novels', we can find 'in all their clarity' the 'structures that writing blurs and dissimulates through the work of putting into [literary] form' (*RoA*, 29). In 'L'Invention de la vie d'artiste' (The Invention of the Life of the Artist) (1975), the article in which he had offered his first detailed reading of *Sentimental Education*, Bourdieu had reproduced an excerpt from Flaubert's notebooks in a text box entitled 'Before Euphemization'.[5] In this early article, as in his subsequent work, Bourdieu plays on the twin meanings of the word 'forme' and its plural 'formes' in French, the first meaning simply 'form' and the second 'social niceties', 'conventions' or 'formalities', to suggest that the act of giving literary form to any utterance (*mettre en forme*) is equivalent to observing the social niceties and formalities, even to putting on airs and graces (*mettre des formes*). As he puts it in *The Rules of Art*, 'to put into form is also to respect the formalities [*mettre en forme, c'est aussi mettre des formes*], and the denial that literary expression performs is what permits the limited manifestation of a truth which, put otherwise, would be unbearable' (*RoA*, 32).

Thus Bourdieu concludes that by dint of being written in the form of a fictional novel, Flaubert's 'socioanalysis' of his own social trajectory was necessarily mediated or refracted through the constraints inherent to the field of literary production. As a result, the 'expressive intention' behind that 'socioanalysis' had to be put into literary form and to respect the formalities and niceties of the literary field, in order to be recognized as literature at all. Through this process, what might, in sociological discourse, have constituted a straightforwardly objective account of the social world became euphemized to such an extent that the objective truths contained in Flaubert's novel were concealed by the very form in which they were expressed. As Bourdieu puts it:

> The work of writing is applied here to a *form*, the structure of the ruling class (or, what comes to the same thing, the *impossible* position of Flaubert in that structure), which it reproduces *in another form*, that is to say transformed in conformity with the laws of the literary field (what are commonly called the laws of a genre or style). This other form which, subjected to the transformative laws of another field, could have expressed itself in a series of concepts, presents itself here in the form of a group of fictional characters, inserted into a story and linked by relations (in the sense of interactions) of which the most visible are sentimental. One can only understand this transformed expression, that is to say the literary work, if one grasps at once the expressive intention (...) and the law of transformation which precisely defines the field in which and for which that literary work is produced. (*Inv*, 92)

According to Bourdieu, this 'work of writing' is strictly analogous to the Freudian dreamwork in that it expresses a repressed (social) truth in a form which simultaneously reveals and conceals or euphemizes that repressed truth. In the case of Flaubert, the work of writing *Sentimental Education* represented the only way in which he could sublimate his particular 'social phantasy', that of occupying a space distant from and uncompromised by the grubby worlds of politics and the market, a phantasy contingent upon the inherited wealth that allowed him to turn his back on those worlds. This, then, is Flaubert's specific 'contradiction'; his disdain for the world of money is contingent upon his inherited wealth. This repressed truth returns in the euphemized form of *Sentimental Education*. To quote Bourdieu, in what is surely one of his most dense and recursive passages:

> The work necessary in order to transform a social phantasy — or, in other cases, a sexual phantasy — into a literary discourse (...) is what allows Flaubert symbolically to master the contradiction that is at the core of his vision of the world. But sublimation is not socioanalysis and Flaubert can only re-appropriate for himself the form which organizes his perception of the social world and of his position in that world in a *misrecognizable* form. As the product of being put into form and of respecting the formalities [*de la mise en forme et du respect des formes*], this form demands to be appreciated with all due respect to the social niceties [*selon les formes et dans les formes*], that is to say as a form. By only saying what he says in a form which tends to suggest he is not saying it (according to the logic of denial), the writer calls for a formal (or formalist) reading which recognizes and reproduces the initial denial instead of negating it in order to dis-cover what it is that is being denied. The circle of collective misrecognition closes when the

content which the form denies is, as it were, *re-misrecognized*, that is recognized and understood in terms of its form alone, the form in which it expresses itself by denying itself. (*Inv*, 92)

Literary form thus functions on two levels to euphemize and conceal the very truths it reveals. Through the mediating force of a field of literary *production*, Flaubert's 'expressive intention' is forced into the euphemistic forms proper to literature. Secondly and thereafter, the truths euphemized through literary form are 're-misrecognized' in the field of literary *reception* by professional literary critics, who interpret the work primarily or exclusively in terms of the very literary form which conceals literature's repressed social truths. Hence, in the 'Invention de la vie d'artiste' article, Bourdieu presents a selection of earlier critical readings of *Sentimental Education* in a section entitled 'Re-Misrecognition' (*Inv*, 76–7). These serve as evidence of the mediating force exerted by the field of literary reception, of the role it plays in further euphemizing Flaubert's expressive intention and closing the circle of collective mis-recognition, as it were.

In *The Rules of Art* Bourdieu therefore argues that Flaubert's novel would represent a socioanalysis of the novelist's own position in the social field were it not for the mediating and euphemizing force of the literary field, which ensures that *Sentimental Education*'s content is expressed in a form which conceals the very truths it reveals. As Bourdieu puts it, 'the vision of the field of power' Flaubert offers in his novel could be called sociological 'if it were not separated from a scientific analysis by the form in which it at once delivers and masks itself'. He goes on:

In fact, *Sentimental Education* reconstitutes in an extraordinarily exact manner the structure of the social world in which it was produced and even the mental structures which, fashioned by those social structures, are the generating principle of the work in which those structures are revealed. But it does so with its own specific means, that is to say by giving to be *seen* and *felt*, in exemplifications or, better, in evocations, in the strong sense of incantations capable of producing effects, notably on the *body*, through the 'evocationary magic' of words able to 'speak to the sensibility' and to obtain a belief and an imaginary participation *analogous* to that we normally grant the real world. (*RoA*, 31–2)

In order to understand the incantatory powers Bourdieu attributes to literary form here, its apparent ability to 'talk to the sensibility' and exert effects directly on the body, it is necessary to bear in mind the properly aesthetic characteristics he also attributes to the habitus.

The habitus, as Bourdieu theorizes it, is an incorporated structure of pre-discursive dispositions and practical anticipations, of ways of seeing the world and being in it. Like the aesthetic in Kant's *Third Critique*, the habitus mediates between the realms of objective social necessity and subjective sentiment; it is the structure in which the imperatives of the social field become entwined with each agent's deepest sentiments, affections, and dispositions. If the habitus plays a role in reproducing existing social relations, it is precisely because of its ability to ensure that the objective imperatives of the social world are in accord with each agent's subjective dispositions, affects, and expectations. So, for example, the low objective chances of someone from a working-class background gaining access to an elite higher education institution become internalized to form part of a working-class habitus which will tend to reject higher education as being 'not for the likes of us'. The habitus hence possesses a structure that is simultaneously temporal and aesthetic; it generates a sense both of what can practically be anticipated and what feels right, in accordance with its incorporated structure of expectations, sentiments and affects. The habitus will thus produce a set of relatively predictable actions or practices that may appear to be freely chosen but are nonetheless endowed with a characteristic purposefulness without purpose. Such practices are, to quote *The Logic of Practice* (1990 [1980]), 'informed by a kind of objective finality without being consciously organized in relation to an explicitly constituted end; intelligible and coherent without springing from an intention of coherence and deliberate decision; adjusted to the future without being the product of a project or plan'.[6] As Jonathan Loesberg was the first to point out, habitus and practice are figured at such moments as being strictly analogous to the Kantian aesthetic object, 'read as that most familiar of literary objects, the organic whole that operates purposively without purpose'.[7]

To return to *Sentimental Education*, Bourdieu's point is that if this novel both reveals and conceals objective social structures, this is because it re-naturalizes the objective structures it reveals through the workings of a literary form that re-aestheticizes those structures in a manner that is strictly analogous to the workings of the habitus. By dint of its literary form, the novel presents the structures it reveals both in the form of a logical temporal order or chronology that naturalizes those events and in an aesthetic form that appeals to the embodied sentiments and affects that are at the core of the habitus. There is, for Bourdieu, a strict analogy between the suspension of disbelief undergone by readers of literary fiction and agents' uncritical investment in the apparent self-evidence of the broader social field. The 'reality effect' achieved by novelists in the realm of fiction, by means of literary form, is thus analogous to the much wider 'reality effect' which habitus and practice achieve, through their aesthetic structure, in the social field as a whole. Social reality, according to Bourdieu, is experienced as though it had the form of fiction. The role of the sociologist is to puncture that reality effect and reveal the hidden truths it conceals, both as regards the fictional illusions generated in the literary field and the social illusions generated in the social field. As he puts it: 'To objectify the novelistic illusion, and especially the relationship to the so-called real world it supposes, is to remind ourselves that the reality against which we measure all fictions is merely the recognized referent of an (almost) universally shared illusion' (*RoA*, 33–4).

At this point in his analysis, therefore, Bourdieu appears to set up a simple dichotomy between literary form, on the one hand, and sociological reason, on the other. The role of any sociological reading of a literary text is to 'break the charm' by suspending 'the complicity which unites author and reader in the same relation of denial of the reality expressed by the text'. The sociological reading can thus 'reveal the truth that the text enunciates, but in such a way that it does not say it' (*RoA*, 32). In the opening sections of *The Rules of Art*, Bourdieu argues that it is precisely this ability to break through the forms of denial inherent to literary form that distinguishes his sociology of literature from the work of professional literary critics. Such critics, he maintains, tend to produce idealist and ahistorical readings of literature, notably through their 'pure interest in pure form'. His sociology of literature will avoid the pitfalls inherent in such formalist interpretations by attending to the material conditions of a literary work's production, reconstructing the coordinates of the literary field within which literary texts are produced. This will allow him to uncover 'an expressive drive which the putting–into–form imposed by the social necessity of the field tends to render unrecognizable' (*RoA*, xviii). The role of sociology thus appears to be to strip away the euphemizing carapace of literary form in order to uncover the denied or repressed truths that form conceals. This will be achieved by reconstructing the coordinates of a field of literary production seen as responsible for imposing that form on any author's 'expressive drive'.

It is this apparent dichotomy between literary form and sociological truth that Leenhardt criticizes, arguing that it relies on a series of questionable binary oppositions between the literary realm of sensuality, magic and embodied belief, on the one hand, and sociological reason, on the other (Leenhardt, 265–7). However, Leenhardt overlooks one possibility inherent to the analogy Bourdieu draws between literary form and the aesthetic structure of the habitus. For if the habitus plays its role in reproducing the status quo largely on account of its aesthetic structure, then it would seem to follow that certain radical aesthetic forms might be able to disrupt the normal smooth functioning of the habitus by delivering a shock to the structures of perception and sentiment incorporated within it. This is a possibility Bourdieu appears to concede somewhat later in his analysis of Flaubert's fiction in *The Rules of Art*. Somewhat confusingly, however, he attributes this defamiliarizing potential to *Sentimental Education*, the very novel whose form, he had earlier argued, worked to conceal the truths it revealed. Here Bourdieu argues that Flaubert's writing style should be designated a kind of 'realist formalism', inasmuch as its formal complexity is precisely what allows Flaubert to achieve 'the evocation of this real which is more real than the sensory appearances given over to a straightforwardly realist description' (*RoA*, 108). If Flaubert's fiction can generate this 'reality effect much more profound than the one that analysts normally designate by the name', this is because through its very sensory form it functions to defamiliarize apparently self-evident social conventions and assumptions by making them felt again or anew. As he puts it:

To make of writing a quest at once formal and material which aims to inscribe, in those words which are most capable, by their very form, of evoking it, the intensified experience of the real that they contributed to producing in the mind of the writer himself, is to oblige the reader to tarry over the sensory form of the text, a visible and sonic material, loaded with correspondences with the real, which are situated both in the order of meaning and the order of the sensory, rather than skating over that form, as though it were a transparent sign, read without being seen, to go directly to its meaning. This is also hence to force the reader to discover there the intensified vision of the real which has been inscribed there by the incantatory evocation implied in the work of writing. (*RoA*, 109)

Literary form here is read in apparently classically modernist terms as possessing a defamiliarizing potential. Form is attributed the capacity to make felt all of the dispositions, the sentiments, the categories of thought and action that normally remain at the level of the unspoken or the implicit, incorporated in a purely 'practical state' into the structures of Flaubert's habitus. Thus literary form can produce a kind of 'anamnesis' by bringing the previously implicit, practical schemes of the habitus to the level of an objective discourse communicated through a sensory form. To quote Bourdieu again, 'it is through this work on form that certain structures are projected into the novel, those structures which the writer, like every social agent, carries within himself in practical state, without truly mastering them. Through this work on form is achieved the anamnesis of everything that ordinarily remains buried, in implicit or unconscious state, underneath the automatisms of an emptily revolving language' (*RoA*, 108).

As we have seen, at certain points in *The Rules of Art* Bourdieu argues that Flaubert's fiction exploits its literary form to produce a 'reality effect' which is strictly analogous to the reality effects produced in the broader social field through the workings of habitus and practice. Here, however, he seems to suggest that through its very formal complexity Flaubert's fiction forestalls that conventional reality effect through a process of defamiliarization which manages 'to obtain from the reader, by the power specific to writing, this intensified gaze on an intensified representation of the real, and of a real methodically rejected by the ordinary conventions and proprieties' (*RoA*, 109). The equivalence Bourdieu had earlier drawn between Flaubert's use of literary form (*mettre en forme*) and his consequent submission to the formalities and social niceties of the literary field (*mettre des formes*) seems to have broken down here. Far from being the expression of a necessary submission to social convention, Flaubert's form is now identified as that which expresses and permits the rejection of such convention and hence the defamiliarization of convention's apparent self-evidence.

It is difficult to see how these two accounts of the function of Flaubert's literary form can be reconciled. In the first account, the task of the sociologist of literature is to strip away the euphemizing carapace of literary form to uncover Flaubert's unvarnished expressive intention, for example by studying the notebooks in which that intention was articulated 'before euphemization'. In this account, literary form is interpreted as a force of euphemization and an expression of the structural constraints imposed on any author by the literary field to respect the forms and niceties of the literary institution. To seek to interpret a literary work without taking the constraining and mediating force exerted by the literary field into account can only, Bourdieu implies, contribute to the 're-misrecognition' of the truths that literature simultaneously reveals and conceals. As we have seen, this is the argument he advances both in the opening sections of *The Rules of Art* and in the article, 'L'Invention de la vie d'artiste', when he maintains that the 'circle of collective misrecognition closes when the content which the form denies is, as it were, *re-misrecognized*, that is recognized and understood in terms of its form alone, the form in which it expresses itself by denying itself' (*Inv*, 92).

The second account Bourdieu offers of the role of literary form in *The Rules of Art* seems to contradict everything he has previously argued. Here Flaubert's literary form is not a force for euphemizing such truths; it is, on the contrary, the defamiliarizing force that allows those truths to be felt. Far from concealing sociological truths, literary form is precisely what enables the reader to feel those truths for themselves and this without the need for a sociologist to intervene to 'break the charm' which unites reader and novelist in their complicit denial of the repressed truths a novel such as *Sentimental Education* contains in euphemized form. If Flaubert's form can do all of this on its own, we might wonder what precise role the sociologist has to play here, not least since the defamiliarizing potential of literature was first theorized by literary critics, rather than sociologists.

Implicit confirmation of the superfluity of the sociologist here is provided by Bourdieu's reading, in *The Rules of Art*, of William Faulkner's short story, 'A Rose for Emily'. In his contribution to this special number, John Speller offers a more detailed analysis of this reading. For our purposes, it is sufficient to note that Bourdieu attributes to the formal characteristics of Faulkner's short story the capacity to force its readers to reflect upon and question the conventions of linear narrative and, through that, to question their uncritical investment in the apparent self-evidence of social convention and hierarchy (*RoA*, 322–9). At no point in his reading of 'A Rose for Emily' does Bourdieu suggest that Faulkner's form simultaneously works to conceal the social truths it thus reveals. Nor does he argue that the form employed in that short story was imposed on Faulkner by the constraints of a literary field which demanded the writer's expressive intention be 'put into form and respect the formalities' of the literary institution. Indeed, Bourdieu makes no attempt to situate Faulkner within the American literary field of his day or to read his short story as being in any way influenced, whether in its form or its content, by the structuring force of that field. In short, Bourdieu's reading of Faulkner's short story would seem to contradict his own strictures regarding the necessity for the sociologist to historicize the conditions of a literary text's production in order to avoid reproducing the idealist, formalist, and ahistorical kinds of literary reading typically produced by literary critics. In his reading of 'A Rose for Emily' Bourdieu thus seems happy to attribute a meaning and political potential to Faulkner's short story entirely independent of any consideration of the mediating force of either its original field of production or its contemporary field of reception, much less of the 'collective mis-recognition' those two fields supposedly engender, should they remain unanalysed.

There seems to be one further problem in Bourdieu's account of the kinds of truth contained in Flaubert's novel and of the role of literary form in either concealing or revealing that truth. As we have seen, Bourdieu is, at various points in his analysis, keen to posit a direct analogy between 'the work of writing' and the Freudian dreamwork. He argues that it is through the work of writing that certain repressed social truths come to be at once revealed and concealed in Flaubert's fiction. The analogy he is drawing with psychoanalysis is made much more explicit in his work on Martin Heidegger, where Bourdieu identifies the same logic of revelation and concealment at work behind the properly philosophical form of Heidegger's writings, a form which serves to euphemize the repressed truth of the philosopher's extreme right-wing political affiliations. In this instance, Bourdieu illustrates this apparently contradictory dialectic of revelation and concealment by reference to the joke first told by Sigmund Freud and repeated by Jacques Lacan to explain the functioning of repressed desire, language and the Symbolic Order in his 'Seminar on the "Purloined Letter"': 'Why are you lying to me by telling me you're going to Krakow so that I'll believe you're going to Lemberg, when in fact you're going to Krakow?'.[8] Thus Bourdieu argues that the repression of social truths through the work of literary or philosophical writing functions analogously to the repression of unspeakable desires in the Freudo-Lacanian unconscious.

At other points, however, Bourdieu offers a rather different account of the nature of the truths contained in literature, an account that seems incompatible with these psychoanalytic conceptions of repression and the unconscious. At such moments, he argues that these truths correspond to the schemes of perception, structures of feeling, thought and action incorporated into Flaubert's habitus at the practical, implicit, hence unconscious level. These correspond to 'those structures which the writer (. . .) carries within himself in practical state' and whose 'anamnesis' is accomplished by Flaubert's 'work on form' (*RoA*, 108). It is important to remember that the incorporation or internalization of social imperatives or of accepted ways of seeing the world and acting in it is not at all the same as the repression of unpalatable truths and desires in the unconscious, as

Freud understands it. The habitus, for Bourdieu, represents a socially determined set of practical categories of thought and action, the socially generated matrix through which every agent perceives and makes sense of the social world. Whilst those categories of perception may be unconscious, in the general sense of existing beyond the immediate grasp of the conscious mind, they are in no way analogous to the unconscious as Freud understands it.

For Freud, the unconscious is the site of everything that precisely *resists incorporation*, of repressed desires and drives whose return, in the form of jokes, slips of the tongue, or inconsistencies, threatens to shatter the kind of stable schemes of feeling and perception Bourdieu locates in the incorporated structures of the habitus. Repression of unconscious desires or unpalatable truths, in the Freudian sense, is thus definitely *not* analogous to the incorporation and naturalization of schemes of thought and action, as Bourdieu understands it. Inasmuch as some truths might logically be seen to be repressed in Bourdieu's account of the social world, these would correspond not to the incorporated schemes of the habitus but rather to the knowledge that those schemes are not natural or universal but socially determined and historically arbitrary. The return of the repressed in the realm of legitimate taste, for example, would thus involve acknowledging that the incorporated schemes of perception that distinguish between the refined and the vulgar, the subtle and the crude, the high and the low are not universal criteria of judgement at all but socially determined oppositions whose objective function is to naturalize and reproduce class distinctions. The return of the repressed would thus correspond to what shatters the practical schemes of the habitus, not to what renders those practical, implicit schemes explicit, locating in them the objective truth of the social world.

In his readings of *Sentimental Education*, however, Bourdieu frequently suggests that it is the incorporated schemes of thought and action contained in Flaubert's habitus that correspond to the repressed truth of his fiction, a repressed truth that is revealed and concealed, to varying degrees, by the workings of literary form. Thus throughout his analyses of literature, Bourdieu constantly slips between notions of repression and incorporation, conflating these two distinct concepts. By extension, he also alternates between two seemingly incompatible accounts of the role of literary form. According to the first account, form is what controls the return of repressed social truths. As he puts it: 'the unveiling finds its limits in the fact that the writer retains in some way the control of the return of the repressed. The putting-into-form he enacts is like a generalized euphemism' (*RoA*, 32). According to the second account, literary form is what accomplishes the 'anamnesis' of the truths incorporated, in practical form, into any author's habitus: 'should we not ask ourselves if the work on form is not what makes possible the partial anamnesis of deep and repressed structures?' (*RoA*, 3–4). Just as repression and incorporation are not analogous procedures, so the return of the repressed and anamnesis are conceptually quite distinct.

The original example of anamnesis is found in the parable of the young slave in Plato's *Meno*. Here Socrates is shown using the process of 'maeutics' to uncover and render explicit the young slave's previously implicit and purely practical knowledge of the laws of geometry. Bourdieu himself has described his own practice of sociology as being modelled on this Socratic procedure of anamnesis:

In order to explain what I have to say in sociology, I could use the parable of Socrates and the little slave. I think that the sociologist is someone who, at the cost of a labour of enquiry and interrogation, using modern means and techniques, helps others give birth to something they know without knowing it.[9]

It is this procedure of anamnesis that Bourdieu employs in his readings of *Sentimental Education*, when he seeks to demonstrate that Flaubert's novel contains in practical or implicit form objective truths about the social world, truths that express the practical schemes of perception incorporated into the novelist's own habitus. According to this model of anamnesis, Flaubert's novel is taken to contain an ideal core of meaning which reflects the logic of the social world which produced it, a logic mediated both through the habitus of the novelist and the structural constraints of the field of literary production.

Despite Bourdieu's claims to the contrary, the hidden truths contained in the novel are in no way understood in terms analogous to a Freudian account of repression and the unconscious. A coherent application to literary study of the Freudian conceptions of repression and the unconscious would surely result in something like Pierre Macherey's *Theory of Literary Production* (1966), where the repressed truth of social antagonism is seen to return in the literary text in the form of a series of logical inconsistencies, textual blanks and narrative contradictions.[10] Bourdieu's contention that Flaubert's novel contains a 'quasi-scientific' objectification of mid–nineteenth-century French society is much closer to the work of Georg Lukács, in this respect. For what is at stake for Bourdieu, as for Lukács, is fiction's ability faithfully or objectively to represent the totality of social relations at any given historical moment. Each thinker offers a diametrically opposed assessment of the value of Flaubert's fiction in this regard and each has a different understanding of the process whereby the totality or objectivity of the social field comes to be expressed in literary form. Yet they both value literature above all for its ability to offer, in Bourdieu's terminology, an objectification of the social world. It is this that explains Shiach's complaint that, in his work on 'masculine domination', Bourdieu treats *To the Lighthouse* 'as a series of descriptions' rather than a text that might 'offer a formal challenge' to the gendered practical schemes of thought and action that determine Mr Ramsay's behaviour in the novel. For what Bourdieu will credit that novel with achieving, through its 'work of writing', is precisely the 'anamnesis' of the ordinarily implicit schemes of thought and action incorporated into the habitus of a dominant male.[11]

As we have seen, Bourdieu attributes a central role to literary form in his account of narrative fiction's ability to reveal objective truths about that social world. However, he seems to offer a range of different, if not simply contradictory accounts both of the precise role played by form here and the specific nature of the truths it can uncover. In one account, Flaubert's form works analogously to the Freudian dreamwork to encode and hence euphemize the repressed truths it simultaneously reveals and conceals. In another account, Flaubert's form is what achieves the work of anamnesis by making the reader feel anew all that was previously implicit or taken for granted. In one account, the truth repressed through Flaubert's form corresponds to his inherited wealth and status, the disavowed condition of possibility of a habitus which looks disdainfully down on the world of money on which it depends. In another account, that repressed truth corresponds to the practical schemes of perception and appreciation incorporated within Flaubert's habitus, which can be rendered explicit through anamnesis. Bourdieu's understanding of literary form thus appears caught between the incompatible logics of repression and incorporation, symptomatic interpretation and anamnesis. It is tempting to interpret such contradictions as themselves symptoms of the repressed truth underpinning Bourdieu's own sociological habitus, as well as the 'social necessity' of the sociological field within which he works. That sociological habitus and field could be seen as working together to produce schemes of perception and appreciation according to which literature is relegated to a realm of, at best, 'quasi-scientific' truths, against which the domain of sociological science and reason defines itself. The truth that such a sociological habitus must repress is the knowledge that, as Jacques Rancière has pointed out, sociology's pretension to offer an objective account of a society, its citizens, morals, institutions and culture was first realized in the work of novelists such as Victor Hugo and Honoré de Balzac.[12] Scientific sociology, from Durkheim on, has thus always been parasitic on the literary forms against which it seeks to define itself. The vicissitudes and contradictions of Bourdieu's accounts of literary form might thus be interpreted as a disavowed acknowledgement of that repressed truth, a return of the repressed that shatters the schemes of perception incorporated into his sociological habitus, according to which the sociologist seeks to 'quite simply look things in the face and see them as they are',[13] whilst the literary critic falls victim to 'the idealism of literary hagiography' (*RoA*, xvi).

NOTES

1 Toril Moi, 'Appropriating Bourdieu: Feminist Theory and Pierre Bourdieu's Sociology of Culture', *New Literary History* 22:4 (1991), 1017–49 (1040).

2 Jacques Leenhardt, '*Les Règles de l'art* de Pierre Bourdieu', *French Cultural Studies* 4:12 (1993), special number *Pierre Bourdieu*, edited by Jill Forbes and Michael Kelly, 263–70. Subsequent references to this article will be to 'Leenhardt' in parentheses in the text.

3 Morag Shiach, 'Cultural Studies and the Work of Pierre Bourdieu', *French Cultural Studies* 4:12 (1993), special number *Pierre Bourdieu*, edited by Jill Forbes and Michael Kelly, 213–23 (221).

4 Pierre Bourdieu, *The Rules of Art: Genesis and Structure of the Literary Field,* translated by Susan Emanuel (Cambridge: Polity Press, 1996), 103. Subsequent references to this work will be to *RoA* in parentheses in the text. All translations have been modified.

5 Pierre Bourdieu, 'L'Invention de la vie d'artiste', *Actes de la recherche en sciences sociales* 2 (1975), 65–93 (84). Subsequent references to this article will be to *Inv* in parentheses in the text. All translations are my own.

6 Pierre Bourdieu, *The Logic of Practice,* translated by Richard Nice (Cambridge: Polity Press, 1990), 50–1.

7 Jonathan Loesberg, 'Bourdieu and the Sociology of Aesthetics', *English Literary History* 60:4 (1993), 1033–56 (1039).

8 Pierre Bourdieu, *The Political Ontology of Martin Heidegger,* translated by Peter Collier (Cambridge: Polity Press, 1991), 85.

9 Pierre Bourdieu, *Si le monde social m'est supportable, c'est parce que je peux m'indigner,* entretien avec Antoine Spire (La Tour d'Aigues: Editions de l'aube, 2002), 14–15.

10 Pierre Macherey, *A Theory of Literary Production*, translated by Geoffrey Wall (London: Routledge & Kegan Paul, 1978).

11 Pierre Bourdieu, *Masculine Domination*, translated by Richard Nice (Cambridge: Polity Press, 2001), 69.

12 Jacques Rancière, *La Parole muette, Essai sur les contradictions de la littérature* (Paris: Hachette Littératures, 1998), 43–52.

13 For reasons unknown, the sentence from which this phrase has been taken does not appear in the English translation of *The Rules of Art*.

Reading and Reflexivity: Bourdieu's Faulkner

John Speller

Abstract:

A rarely examined internal reading by Bourdieu at the end of *The Rules of Art* of William Faulkner's short story 'A Rose for Emily' provides the starting point for a reflection on Bourdieu's theories of reading and reflexivity. The article begins by looking at Bourdieu's theory of literary reception, and its identification of two distinct modalities of reading, 'scholastic' and 'naive'. It then places Bourdieu's discussion of 'A Rose for Emily' as a 'reflexive' text in the context of his wider theory of reflexivity. Bourdieu's approach to reading Faulkner's text is compared with those deployed elsewhere by more established literary critics, notably Jean-Paul Sartre and Roland Barthes. Finally, the question of how his internal reading fits within the logic of a theoretical work devoted to the 'reflexive' practice and method of field analysis is discussed.

Keywords: Pierre Bourdieu, William Faulkner, reflexivity, reading, double historicization, 'A Rose for Emily'

Tucked away at the end of *The Rules of Art,* is a reading by Pierre Bourdieu of William Faulkner's short story 'A Rose for Emily'.[1] Rarely remarked on by critics, this analysis is interesting for several reasons. Most strikingly, it is an *internal reading* of a text at the end of a work that has spent most of its length extolling field analysis, and chiding other modes of reading, from New Criticism to structuralism and deconstruction, for failing to position works in their socio-historical contexts. Indeed, it could be seen as demonstrating effectively what a good 'internal' reading can do on its own terms: it provides a key not only for understanding the text we are reading, but also the very process by which we come to an understanding of that text. Bourdieu's argument is that Faulkner's short story is designed as

Paragraph 35.1 (2012): 83–96
DOI: 10.3366/para.2012.0043
© Edinburgh University Press
www.eupjournals.com/para

a sort of prompt for the reader to engage in just such a reflection and auto-reflection. This article will take us through Bourdieu's analysis of the structure of 'A Rose for Emily' and how it plays on our unquestioned assumptions and expectations, only then to send us back to examine those same techniques and presuppositions. Along the way, Bourdieu's approach to reading this text will be compared with those deployed elsewhere by more established literary critics, notably Jean-Paul Sartre and Roland Barthes. In the end, we should arrive at a closer understanding both of this neglected chapter in *The Rules of Art,* and of its relevance, despite initial appearances, to the overall economy of Bourdieu's thought on literature.

Reading

Bourdieu's analysis of 'A Rose for Emily' centres on his contention that it leads readers to question and reflect on the background assumptions and habits of thought they bring to their readings of literary texts. Beginning at Miss Emily's funeral, we are given scenes from her life in retrospect, from the point of view of the community of Jefferson, expressed as a disembodied 'we'. Everything appears to be in order, from the nosiness of the female neighbours to the conformity of the men. Miss Emily herself is designated as an eminently respectable personage, and the other townsfolk pay her tribute out of a sense of almost filial piety. She is described as a relic from a bygone era (a 'fallen monument'), a symbol of dying traditions and a more civilized age. It is only at the end of the story that we discover that this 'noble' Miss Emily, whom we had assumed beyond reproach, had murdered her lover and been sharing her bed with his corpse for the previous decades (*RE*, 9–20).

In this sense, Bourdieu describes 'A Rose for Emily' as 'a reflexive story, a reflecting story which encloses in its very structure the program (in the computer sense) for a reflection on the novel and on naive reading' (*RoA*, 325). Having reached the end of the story, we are encouraged to look back or at least mentally recapitulate the tale, to see how our trust had been abused. It is only then that we notice the beguiling 'we' of the narrative voice; the common-sense explanations we are inclined to believe; the blurring of the chronology, which we had assumed to be following a linear structure more common in novels; and the way the author plays on our expectations concerning social conventions and hierarchy (in particular, the idea of nobility).

'A Rose for Emily', then, calls for a double reading in two distinctive modes. The first Bourdieu describes as 'naive', in that it is spontaneous and uncritical. The second is labelled 'scholastic', since it is the mode of reading taught and practised in school. Whereas the first mode of reading tends to be hurried and distracted, a scholastic reading involves taking time to look closely at the nuances of style and technique. Whereas a naive reading proceeds from the beginning to the end of the story, a scholastic reading flicks backwards and forwards, to explore its narrative cohesion (or 'organic unity'). 'A Rose for Emily' plays on both these levels, beguiling us into believing its literary illusion, only then to send us back to see how it had led us astray.

Bourdieu's starting point — for this particular story at least — is rather different to that of Jean-Paul Sartre, who in an essay on temporality in Faulkner argued that Faulkner's readers are likely to be 'first struck by the oddities of the technique'.[2] In particular, Sartre writes that readers of his work are immediately tempted 'to look for landmarks and to reconstruct the chronology for [themselves]'.[3] 'A Rose for Emily' consists of a series of flashbacks, of Emily facing down the town Aldermen over her taxes; of the four men sneaking around to sprinkle lime about her house, to remove the smell and avoid another confrontation; of Emily's father's death; of her romance with Homer Baron; of his disappearance and her eventual death. Bourdieu's point, however, is that in 'A Rose for Emily' Faulkner wished initially to lure us into reading the story in our 'naive', linear way — only then to turn back and try to piece together the order of a chronology that had been studiously distorted and obscured.

Sartre's approach might in some respects be compared to an attitude that Bourdieu challenges elsewhere. He sees a long list of literary critics, from Stanley Fish and Wolfgang Iser to Michael Riffaterre, with their various versions of the 'informed reader' or *archilecteur*, as projecting unduly a very particular reading experience. They take 'as object (. . .) the subjective experience of the work of art which is that of the analyst, meaning of a cultivated person of a certain society, (. . .) without paying attention to the *historicity* of this experience or of the object to which it is applied' (*RoA*, 286). If this 'scholastic error' is so widespread, Bourdieu suggests, it is because the appearance of literary works demanding this mode of reading coincided with the appearance of a corpus of readers with the time and inclination to treat literary language not as a simple medium, but as an object of analysis and contemplation. In fact, Bourdieu argues, the interests of 'pure' literary writers, focusing on form, and those of a body of critics, including professional academics, teachers and students, are mutually reinforcing, as each supplies the demand of the other (*RoA*, 304).

Whereas a scholastic reading is associated with the scholastic setting (which is often ignored by readers, who speak as if their own understanding of the text were universally valid), a 'naive' reading follows the routines and patterns of thought we engage in our everyday lives. Indeed, Bourdieu argues that the basis of what we refer to commonly as 'realism' (or *vraisemblance*) in literature is the 'homology' between the reality represented in the story and the social structures which regiment the world we experience. In *The Rules of Art*, Bourdieu introduces the notion of a belief effect (*effet de croyance*) to describe this phenomenon. He explains it by a fit between the mental structures readers have formed from the habits and routines of everyday life and the underlying structure of the relations between characters (and the associated artefacts and locations) in the narrative. This structure provides the underlying logic of the characters' interactions; and when it is analogous with that which governs our own social interactions, the resulting narrative strikes us as realistic.

In his analysis of 'A Rose for Emily', Bourdieu speaks again of a sort of 'reading contract' between the author and the reader, to designate 'the naive trust that readers place in their reading and the abandoned way they throw themselves into it, along with all their common-sense assumptions' (*RoA*, 324). 'Common sense' is a loaded term in Bourdieu's lexicon, designating both the received ideas of a population, and the quasi-orchestrated practices of habitus conforming to this dominant world view (and which tend therefore to reproduce the social structure through their actions). Faulkner's short story first exploits then shakes its readers from this doxic mindset, in which everything in the world seems to be predictable and to make sense.

Bourdieu seeks to differentiate his belief effect from Barthes's more famous notion of a reality effect (*effet de réel*)—without, however, explaining their differences in detail. We know, nonetheless, that for Barthes it was the 'needless details' (*détails inutiles*) the author includes that strike the reader as realistic, some of his examples being Mme Aubain's barometer in Flaubert's short story 'Un cœur simple', or his description of Rouen in *Madame Bovary*. Barthes argues that these descriptions have no structural or narrative function in the text, except that of simulating reality. For Barthes, such details interrupt the flow of the narrative, and at such moments we are confronted with a fragment of the 'real', in its senseless materiality or 'there-ness':

> The general structure of the narrative (. . .) appears essentially *predictive*; simplifying to the extreme (. . .), one can say that at each articulation of the narrative syntagm, someone says to the hero (or to the reader, whichever): if you act in such or such a way, if you choose such or such an alternative, this is what will happen (. . .). Description is entirely different; it has no predictive function; 'analogical', its structure is purely summative and does not contain this series of choices and alternatives which give the narration the character of a vast *dispatching* with a referential (and not purely discursive) temporality.[4]

In contrast, for Bourdieu it is precisely the thoroughgoing correspondance between the reality represented in the fiction and our everyday world that provides the basis for his belief effect. This shared structure is not revealed directly, as it would be by a 'scientific' analysis as defined by Bourdieu. Instead, it appears (as it does in 'reality') in the *form* of visible actions and interactions, which seem to 'make sense' intuitively, but which can be understood rationally only with reference to the wider structure of relations between people and things. Both literary and sociological texts carry, as it were, the imprint of such structures. But whereas social science would attempt to objectify the system of relations as such, using concepts and theories, literature 'does so with its own specific means, that is, by giving it to be *seen* and *felt* in *exemplifications* (or, better, *evocations* (. . .)) in the "evocatory magic" of words apt to "speak to the sensibilities" and to obtain a belief and an imaginary participation *analogous* to those that we grant to the real world' (*RoA*, 32). An example from 'A Rose for Emily', already mentioned, would be Miss Emily's 'nobility', a status which seems to determine her every behaviour and attribute, notably precluding her marriage to Homer Baron and ruling out the very idea of murder.

While the two terms designate different kinds of textual effect, it would be limiting to oppose them such that one had to choose between one or the other (as Bourdieu perhaps suggests we should). This would grant no room within our experience of a novel for those random elements and 'pure' descriptive passages which, as Barthes argues, can produce a documentary-like effect of realism through our very inability to 'reduce' them semantically. Certainly, 'A Rose for Emily' is remarkably compact, every detail chosen to create an impression or atmosphere. And it is certainly difficult to find any superfluous details in *Sentimental Education*, Flaubert's 'epic without air'. Yet even the most significant detail in the economy of a text cannot be completely reduced to its function in a narrative. There will always remain an excess of meaning and kernel of non-sense in which the thing itself appears.

Comparison with Sartre also helps Bourdieu to bring his ideas into focus. We have seen how the reading considered by Bourdieu is set off from Sartre's reading of Faulkner, which is preoccupied from the outset with 'oddities of technique'. In the case of 'A Rose for Emily', Bourdieu argues that the jumbled time-line is designed precisely *not* to be noticed immediately, and that the chronology is intended only to be reconstituted retrospectively. He also develops Sartre's interpretation of Faulkner's philosophy of time. Sartre argues that in Faulkner's nihilistic, absurdist, apocalyptic world-view man is reduced to being 'a creature deprived of possibilities' and reduced to an inanimate object, which (he imagines), if such things could think, would exist in an eternal present. 'But', Sartre asks, 'is man a thinking nail?' For Sartre, man is not the sum of his misfortunes, as Faulkner maintained, but is always engaged and invested in the future, even if that future is death. Sartre refers to Heidegger's *Being and Time* to say: 'Even if human reality has nothing left "ahead" of it, even if it has "reached the end of the road", its being is still determined by this "anticipation of itself." The loss of all hope, for example, does not remove human reality's possibilities, it is simply "a way of *being* towards these same possibilities."'[5]

Bourdieu's account of temporal experience, and the functioning of narrative schemes therein, is developed in reference to his theory of habitus. It is through this theory that he analyses the internalization of social structures and patterns which, in turn, provide the frame of reference via which we can understand and anticipate the flow of events. Past, present, and future are implicated in the navigation of social space, which crucially requires a sense of timing and rhythm, a 'feel for the game'. Unlike Heidegger's (or Sartre's) *Dasein,* separated from other beings by the prospect of a death that can only be one's own, the habitus and its mode of temporalization is, according to Bourdieu, inherently *social*. It is in relation to others, and in light of our past experiences and interactions (themselves governed by diverse social laws or regularities) that we are positioned and position ourselves, and that we take new positions in anticipation of probable outcomes. Bourdieu writes:

In short, the habitus is the basis of the social structuration of temporal existence, of all the anticipations and the presuppositions through which we practically construct the sense of the world — its signification, but also, inseparably, its orientation towards the still-to-come. This is what Faulkner obliges us to discover by methodically disconcerting the sense of the social game that we apply as much in our experience of the world as in the naive reading of the naive telling of that experience. This sense of the game is also a sense of the history of the game, that is, of the still-to-come which it reads directly into the present state of the game, and which it helps to make happen by orienting itself in relation to it, without having to place it explicitly in a conscious project, and hence to constitute it as a contingent *future*. (*RoA*, 329)

On Bourdieu's reading, temporality in Faulkner figures not as a mean-ingless, discontinuous aggregation of elements, but as a social construct in which pockets of sense and order are created from within chaos.

Yet we might ask ourselves whether the denouement of Faulkner's short story is really as unexpected as Bourdieu would have us believe. Are the anticipatory schemes that the story undoubtedly mobilizes really just those of a 'naive' everyday life with no connection to the 'literary', broadly conceived? With its *mise en scène* of a dilapidated mansion and over-grown graveyard, the story can be quite easily located in a diffuse Gothic tradition; with 'eyes (...) like two small pieces of coal pressed into a lump of dough' (*RE*, 11), Miss Emily herself is a far more sinister character than Bourdieu gives us to expect; and the episode when Miss Emily denies her father's death, and refuses to allow his body to be taken away, foreshadows her holding on to the corpse of Homer Baron. Given the ending, we can understand our sense of suspense and foreboding, and might even go back to analyse the way that Faulkner had built up the tension so successfully, without, however, revealing the cause in the narrative. Nonetheless, Bourdieu's suggestion that the ending of 'A Rose for Emily' is completely unforeseen is unlikely to match the experience of many readers with even a little knowledge of — or informally acquired familiarity with — literary genres. In his enthusiasm to find in Faulkner a support for his theory, we might say, Bourdieu bent the story to make it literarily 'flatter' than it in fact is. This does not invalidate Bourdieu's claims that the short story is constructed so as to draw out a particular kind of readerly reflexivity, but it does suggest the space between a 'naive' and a 'reflexive' reading needs to be construed in a more complex fashion.

Reflexivity

The reflexivity of 'A Rose for Emily' is therefore of the 'reflective' sort (as suggested by the etymology, from the Latin *reflectere,* to bend

or turn back). It is 'A Reflecting Story', to use one of Bourdieu's sub-
headings (*RoA*, 324). Yet this reflection is conceived here resolutely
in relation to the reader, and not in relation to the author, as one
might have expected. It is the reader who is obliged to turn back and
examine his or her own assumptions and preconceptions, as (s)he re-
reads the tale more carefully. This reflexivity seems quite different from
that which Bourdieu describes in earlier chapters of *The Rules of Art*.
Slowly, over the course of centuries, the literary writer had become
a recognizable social figure, and literature a distinctive discourse (as
opposed, for instance, to political or religious writing). The literary
field, at the same time, became more 'reflexive', as a faction of writers
began taking their cues from their peers and precursors rather than
from external ('heteronomous') sources (the edicts of the Church,
the commission of a patron, the demands of the market). A corner
of the literary field (what Bourdieu calls the 'the field of restricted
production') closed in on itself, and literature became an exploration
of its own possibilities and limits (*nomoi*). Reflexivity, in this sense,
is a property of writers in the literary field as a whole, and leaves
its most direct mark on works written with a 'pure' or autonomous
intent.

Bourdieu's analysis of 'A Rose for Emily' is conspicuous for the
absence of such a field perspective (and is, no doubt, the weaker
for it). This does not mean, however, that his formalist reading is
incompatible with the mode of analysis Bourdieu develops in *The
Rules of Art*, which interprets the properties of literary works, including
styles and themes, in terms of their authors' positions in the literary
field, previous trajectories, and the position of the literary field in the
field of power. Indeed, it would be quite easy to link the 'reflecting'
character of Faulkner's short story to its social and historical conditions
of production, and Bourdieu himself gives us some hints and guidance
on how to do so. The very structure of 'A Rose for Emily', Bourdieu
writes, calls for that

> extra-ordinary reader, the 'arch-reader', as some used to say (without ever
> questioning the social conditions of possibility of this curious figure), or, better
> still, the *meta-reader* who will know how to read not only the narrative, quite
> simply, but the ordinary reading of the narrative. (*RoA*, 325)

Bourdieu does question the 'social institution' of 'pure' reading,
'which is the end result of a whole history of the field of cultural
production, a history of the production of the pure writer — and the
pure consumer whom the field helps to produce by producing for that

person' (*RoA*, 302). The emergence of reflexive writers, and that of a battery of professional readers, publishers, scholars and other writers, are part of the same process, the two forming an enchanted circle in which each provides the *raison d'être* for the other.

The structure of 'A Rose for Emily' can therefore be associated with the social conditions in which it was written, an advanced state of the literary field. And these conditions being the same as those which are required for a 'reflexive' reading, the author and reader are linked by a shared culture. What is more, Bourdieu writes, one 'does not need to push the empirical observation very far to discover that the reader called for by pure works is the product of exceptional social conditions which reproduce (*mutatis mutandis*) the social conditions of their production (in this sense, the author and legitimate reader are interchangeable)' (*RoA*, 302). Pure readings of pure works require the same frames of literary references and conceptual understanding that shaped the writing of the work itself, and require the same privileged conditions to be cultivated. In this respect, the writer and the reader are the same — or to use Bourdieu's more precise terms, their positions in social space are homologous.

Of course, this is only the most cursory 'double historicization' of 'A Rose for Emily'. A more complete analysis of Faulkner would need to plot literature's status in American society (in what Bourdieu calls the 'field of power'), Faulkner's position relative to other writers in the literary field, and his (familial, educational, financial) trajectory to that point, to understand his choice of form, theme and genre. Similarly, one would need to research the reader's educational background, not forgetting the divergences across time and cultures and between the fields of production and reception. Modern readers may have lost sight of less illustrious writers and works, who and which nevertheless exerted an influence, if only negative, or a less conscious 'field-effect', on Faulkner, while texts can take on new significance when they are transposed into another national culture. Already, we can see though that the history of how the text has achieved its legitimate status in our society and that of the legitimate reader's response are intertwined.

Where does this leave Bourdieu's reading of Faulkner? With increasing insistence from the 1980s, Bourdieu presented his own sociology as 'reflexive', a word that appears in the titles of two of his most 'theoretical' works, *Science de la science et réflexivité* (2001) and *Invitation to a Reflexive Sociology* (1992).[6] He goes so far as to identify reflexivity as perhaps the most defining characteristic of his work: 'I believe that if the sociology I propose differs in any way from the other sociologies of the past and of the present, it is above all in that it *continually turns back onto itself the weapons it produces*.[7] When Bourdieu studied his native region of Béarn in *The Bachelors' Ball* (2002), the French system of *grandes écoles* in *The State Nobility* (1989), or even French culture in general, in *Distinction* (1979), he was simultaneously analysing the society and culture of which he was a product, and to which he owed his own system of dispositions, thoughts, and perceptions (his habitus).[8]

This sociological 'reflexive return' is no less operational in an historical work like *The Rules of Art*. Bourdieu was part of the intellectual tradition of Flaubert, Zola and Sartre, whose precedents he followed, and in many of whose values he believed. Then again, his involvement in that intellectual universe also made him subject to all sorts of blind spots, prejudices and unspoken interests, which sociological study, conceived of as a form of 'auto-socio-analysis', brought to light. Like Proust excavating lost time and memories, Bourdieu's study of the history of the intellectual field was also in part a work of 'unforgetting', or *anamnesis*, digging up his own structuring 'historical unconscious': the story of how his own position as an intellectual, the associated dispositions, categories, concepts and interests (which he shared with his antecedents), how the works he read and the manifold institutions that surrounded him came into being. Bourdieu thought that this sort of research could provide some measure of control over the 'structures of thought and action' he and others had internalized from the experience of inhabiting a particular intellectual field and position, and that this would give him a 'margin of liberty' and critical distance from the dispositions and determinations which, if ignored, could lead to errors or biases in his thinking.

Finally, Bourdieu asks for his own texts to be read 'reflexively': for his readers to turn back and examine their own points of view, using the method demonstrated in his works, before turning away or pronouncing judgement (*RoA*, 342). What this means concretely is they can apply the knowledge and concepts contained in Bourdieu's work to their own particular social contexts, looking for parallels and correlates in their own experience. Bourdieu contrasts this approach to 'theoretical' readings of his work, which only compare his texts with other texts, or which judge them on their internal consistency. This seems to resemble, however, the 'pure' form of literary reading that Faulkner's text encourages; and in fact Bourdieu traces its preponderance in France to the once dominant literary tradition of 'close reading', with its internal analysis and inter-textual comparisons (*RoA*, 193).

Can we therefore conclude that the reflexivity Bourdieu designates as characteristic of his sociology is different in quality, form or degree from that practised by literary writers and critics? One last time, Bourdieu's analysis of Faulkner's short story may help us to find an answer. Indeed, the very fact that his textual analysis turns into sociological reflection on the constructed sense of time and history in itself suggests the two approaches may be complementary. Sociology can assist in the literary critic's task of understanding the literary experience, and literature can give sociologists new insight and ways to express social reality. This was, indeed, one of Bourdieu's assertions (against his critics who claimed that sociology necessarily destroyed or reduced aesthetic pleasure). Bourdieu cites Faulkner as an inspiration for sociologists, to break with the 'biographical illusion' of life-histories as a logical and linear series of events, and common-sense assumptions and preconceptions — illusions that are reinforced by traditional literary narratives. 'This is why', Bourdieu writes in *Raisons pratiques*, 'it is logical to look for assistance to those who have had to break with this tradition on the terrain of its exemplary accomplishment'.[9]

What this shows is that the surprising lack of field analysis in Bourdieu's study of 'A Rose for Emily', or of any more obviously 'self-reflective' comments, is not necessarily in contradiction with his methodological prescriptions. Close reading, of the sort Bourdieu performs, is one of the stages in his more complete theory, which aims to join the techniques of internal reading and external analysis. As in his analysis of Flaubert's *Sentimental Education* in the first part of *The Rules of Art*, Bourdieu begins with an internal analysis of a text, which opens the door to an exploration of the sociological context of writing and reading, which will in turn take us back again to the text. This to-and-fro from the text to the social context and back again, in which each new piece of information and insight reinforces the others and leads to new trails for exploration, could go on indefinitely, Bourdieu writes,

if one did not have to put a stop to it, a rather arbitrary one, in the hope that the first results, provisional and revisable, will have done enough to indicate the direction which should be taken by a social science concerned with converting into a really integrated and cumulative programme of empirical research that legitimate ambition for systematicity which is imprisoned by the totalizing pretensions of 'grand theory'. (*RoA*, 184)

It is therefore left to later researchers to continue the research programme of which the analyses in *The Rules of Art*, in its chapter on Faulkner as elsewhere, are only the beginning, like an initial sketch that needs to be filled in and modified, in a collective work of revision and reflexive reflection.

Concluding Remarks

Bourdieu's analysis of William Faulkner's short story 'A Rose for Emily' is a puzzle at the end of *The Rules of Art*. Having spent much of the rest of his book presenting and demonstrating his theory of cultural fields, Bourdieu offers a purely internal reading of Faulkner's tale, which makes no attempt to link its structure to that of the American literary field in which it was written. Bourdieu sees 'A Rose for Emily' as a spur to reflect on the foundation of the literary illusion, what he calls the *effet de croyance,* that literature can produce. This effect is founded in the analogy between the social world we experience in our ordinary lives and that represented in the narrative, which are organized according to the same patterns and rules. Yet having recounted Miss Emily's life story, the narrator reveals, in the end, her terrible secret, which sends us back to look at (or at least to mentally recapitulate) how the story was told. Only then, according to Bourdieu, do we notice the techniques and devices that Faulkner used to blur the chronology of events and build trust in the narrator and Miss Emily, so that the revelation of her crime is experienced as a shock, despite the clues that appear with hindsight.

In making this argument, Bourdieu engages briefly with Roland Barthes and his theory of the reality effect. Bourdieu opposes his own notion of a belief effect which he claims is more apt, without elaborating his assertion. Yet by concentrating on the fit between our mental structures and the structural principles that lie behind the narrative, Bourdieu seems to have closed his eyes to Barthes's insight that apparently insignificant details and pure descriptions, which cannot be integrated into a meaningful framework, are also part of what can give literary narratives a sense of realism.

Sartre's analyses also enable Bourdieu to mark out the specifity of his approach. Sartre suggests the reader is struck immediately by the oddities of the technique in Faulkner's novels; but for Bourdieu, in 'A Rose for Emily', Faulkner has carefully combined what Barthes might have called a 'readerly' (*lisible*) and a 'writerly' (*scriptible*) text. First, we are to read the short story in our familiar, 'naive' way, as a linear narrative following the usual codes. Then, we are impelled to take an active role in the reconstruction of the 'actual' course of events, and at the same time discover the presuppositions on which Faulkner had played to encourage our initial belief. Elsewhere in Bourdieu's work, we can find an explanation for what might be called Sartre's 'intellectualist bias': his immersion in a scholastic culture of which Faulkner's works are themselves a reflection, and which holds certain 'classic' and 'avant-garde' texts to require a particular mode of formalist reading.

This is not to say, of course, that Bourdieu's reading is without intellectual projections of its own. The sociologist sees the text as a kind of device that demonstrates his own theory of habitus, of the way social structures are internalized as anticipatory dispositions (habitus) which then reproduce those structures through their practices, involving a sense of timing or 'feel for the game'. Not only is it unclear whether Faulkner would have recognized this theory of temporal experience (certainly, it is very different from that which is attributed to him by Sartre). Also, perhaps in his enthusiasm to find in Faulkner a support for his own sociological theories, Bourdieu overlooks the literary techniques of foreshadowing, imagery, and the diffuse Gothic conventions Faulkner employs to create a sense of foreboding, which make the ending less unexpected than Bourdieu claims.

All these reflections are bound up with Bourdieu's notion of reflexivity. It may not be clear initially in what sense 'A Rose for Emily' can be said to be 'reflexive'. On Bourdieu's reading, the short story seems designed to initiate a reflexive return on the part of the reader, who is stimulated to study his or her own response to the text. This appears different from the reflexivity discussed earlier in *The Rules of Art*, which is described as a property of highly autonomous literary fields, which become self-referential. Yet when placed in the context of Bourdieu's broader discussions of reflexivity, we can see that reflexive readers, writers, and literature itself, are products of the same historical process. Bourdieu's sociology provides a framework for the analysis of this sort of eco-system of interdependent, but at the same time distinct and even competing agents and institutions. If he does not undertake such an analysis himself in the particular case of William Faulkner, this is not because the methods of field analysis and close reading are mutually exclusive. Indeed, Bourdieu's theory offers a way to link formalist 'internal' analysis and 'external' sociological contextualization, arguing that the two approaches could be complementary. Perhaps the best approach to Bourdieu's reading of Faulkner is, therefore, to view it as a first attempt, incomplete and flawed, but upon which later critics can build, as part of a collective, reflexive research process.

NOTES

1 Pierre Bourdieu, *The Rules of Art: Genesis and Structure of the Literary Field,* translated by Susan Emanuel (Cambridge: Polity, 1996), 325. Subsequent references to this work will be to *RoA* in parentheses in the text; William Faulkner, 'A Rose for Emily' [1930] in *The Collected Short Stories of William Faulkner* (London: Chatto & Windus, 1963), II, 9–20. Subsequent references to this work will be to *RE* in parentheses in the text.

2 Jean-Paul Sartre, 'À Propos de *Le Bruit et la Fureur.* La temporalité chez Faulkner', in *Situations I* (Paris: Gallimard, 1947), 65–75.

3 Cited in *RoA,* 327.

4 Roland Barthes, 'L'effet de réel' [1968], in R. Barthes et al., *Littérature et réalité* (Paris: Seuil, 1982), 82–90 (83) (my translation).

5 Sartre, 'À Propos de *Le Bruit et la Fureur*', 79–81.

6 Pierre Bourdieu, *Science de la science et réflexivité* (Paris: Raisons d'agir, 2001); Pierre Bourdieu and Loïc J. D. Wacquant, *An Invitation to Reflexive Sociology* (Cambridge: Polity Press, 1992).

7 Bourdieu and Wacquant, *An Invitation to Reflexive Sociology*, 55.

8 See respectively Pierre Bourdieu, *The Bachelors' Ball: The Crisis of Peasant Society in Béarn* [2002], translated by Richard Nice (Cambridge: Polity, 2007); *The State Nobility: Elite Schools in the Field of Power* [1989], translated by Lauretta Clough (Cambridge: Polity, 1996); *Distinction: A Social Critique of the Judgement of Taste* [1979], translated by Richard Nice (London: Routledge, 1984).

9 Pierre Bourdieu, *Raisons pratiques. Sur la théorie de l'action* (Paris: Seuil, 1994), 83 (the chapter in question is not included in the English translation *Practical Reason: On the Theory of Action*, various translators (Cambridge: Polity, 1998)).

Fields and Fragments: Bourdieu, Pascal and the Teachings of Literature

Jeremy Ahearne

Abstract:

Literary pedagogy occupied a privileged place in Bourdieu's early work on education insofar as he saw it as exemplifying in unconscious mode socially segregational dynamics. Bourdieu's expressly 'reductionist' critique was uncannily mirrored, however, by the spread of more economically instrumental approaches to education. Bourdieu's engagement with these led him to develop a fuller apprehension of literature. Yet while the conceptual apparatus he developed can allow the genesis of a literary work in its socio-historical complexity to be grasped more fully, its framing poses significant problems of its own. In particular, its 'hypercontextualizing' injunctions risk stifling ordinary reading practices and the practical pedagogy of canon-formation. Bourdieu's actual practice with literary materials is not bound by these injunctions. His transepochal 'collaboration' with Blaise Pascal, for example, takes place through the insinuation of decontextualised shards of thought into his own writing. The teachings of literature exceed in various ways their scientific framing.

Keywords: Pierre Bourdieu, Blaise Pascal, literature, sociology, education, field theory, fragments

The links between teaching and literatures were a recurrent focus of Bourdieu's thought from the 1960s. Indeed, for much of his writing that nexus appears as a target. Literatures are understood within these domains of his thought in a composite manner, both in the sense of pedagogical corpuses serving class- and nation-based cultural strategies, and as the products of strategies of 'distinction' within increasingly self-conscious and relatively autonomous fractions of an artistic 'field' (the relations between these two dimensions are also explored by Bourdieu). The posture Bourdieu adopts in this

Paragraph 35.1 (2012): 97–114
DOI: 10.3366/para.2012.0044
© Edinburgh University Press
www.eupjournals.com/para

regard is external or 'objectifying': he is the 'scientist' of a society's serious 'games' whose invisible mechanisms need 'explicating'. But Bourdieu is himself implicated in a rather different kind of relation to a 'literature' derived from the processes evoked above but apprehended in a different mode. This relation is largely unthematized as such in his work, but is a constant feature of his thinking practice. Literature here signifies something like a precipitation of dislocated textual fragments whose current status is uncertain (not scientific, not documentary, not immediately instrumental), but which condition and enable certain kinds of perception. Bourdieu, the product of a certain kind of education and self-education, carries them around with him: they are ingrained into his disposition (his *habitus*). They draw out (educt) his understanding in particular ways.

Literature and Social Reproduction

Bourdieu's early critique of literary education (notably in *The Inheritors* and *Reproduction*) can at one level be viewed as a development of Durkheim's classic history of French pedagogy.[1] Durkheim traces how French educational practices, from the Renaissance through the Jesuit colleges and into the nineteenth-century State secondary school apparatus, assigned exorbitant value to the 'literary', or purely verbal, prowess derived from the intensive frequentation of suitably excerpted classical texts. This catered to a stable demand from social elites for the segregative polishing of their offspring, but in Durkheim's view unduly displaced a medieval preoccupation with the things of logic (dialectics) and inhibited an engagement, from the eighteenth century, with the logic of things (natural science). While Durkheim's own notional framework for the purposes of secondary education comprised a nuanced synthesis of these streams, including an important space for the 'literary', his critique of the kind of disposition produced by exclusively literary preoccupations is a powerful leitmotif in his overall account.

Bourdieu's sociological accounts of literary education in the universities of 1960s France echo some of Durkheim's themes. Those teachers and students who invest most intensely in their literary studies tend to apprehend 'reality only indirectly and symbolically, that is, through the veil of rhetorical illusion' (*I*, 50). Certainly, Bourdieu is working through here, as a sociologist, his part in a certain 'conflict of the faculties' (exacerbated perhaps by sociology's 'dominated' location in French universities' faculties of *lettres* prior to 1968).[2] But it is striking that literary pedagogy as such assumes a strategically privileged position in Bourdieu's overall analysis of educational systems. This foreshadows, but only in negative mode, his subsequent argument that, in fact, all agents apprehend reality 'indirectly and symbolically' through a range of 'social fictions', and that literature, as a fiction that declares itself to be fiction, can provide a more probing (though supposedly 'euphemized') representation of this process than accounts which take their epistemic status more seriously.[3] For at this stage, literary study itself is credited by Bourdieu with no part in any such lucidity. If it is particularly revealing, it is so despite itself. It has much to teach, but it cannot itself understand its teachings.

Thus Bourdieu notes that 'if arts students hold a particular place in our analyses, it is because (...) they exhibit in exemplary fashion that relation to culture which we took as our object of study' (*I*, ix; translation modified). For those whose social backgrounds equipped them with the requisite rhetorical lexis and cultural frames of reference, their 'happy' relation to literary syllabuses was 'ratified' rather than 'produced' by the system as it operated (see *I*, 24). At the other extreme, students whose social background equipped them with none of these things entered into an 'unhappy' relation with these syllabuses. The existing 'pedagogy by default' did little to remedy this disjuncture, and its verdicts, at a statistical level, served simply to consolidate it. Indeed the very distance between these students' backgrounds and the arbitrary preciousness of valorized literary culture served to bring out all the more clearly the truth of the educational process as a form of 'acculturation' for these students (*I*, 22). The various charismatic 'mystifications' inherent in the pedagogical relation were 'never more true than in literary teaching', even if they were never absent elsewhere.[4] If literary education evinced such characteristics to a higher degree than other modes of education in the French system, it was because its effective function amounted to little more than '[reproducing] the legitimate culture as it stands and [producing] agents capable of manipulating it legitimately' (*R*, 59).

These analyses were, of course, 'reductive'. At one level, that was their achievement. In a quasi-chemical sense, they reduced through sustained scouring an elaborate growth of belletristic foliage to statistically discernible forms of stratificational functionality. That is not to say the undoubted truths they disclosed were somehow disincarnate. Annie Ernaux has described the 'violent ontological shock' she experienced on assimilating them, and Hélène Merlin-Kajman the 'violent narcissistic wound' that she and other contemporaries endured when coming to terms with these and other works by Bourdieu in the 1960s and 1970s (of course, many mental routines were also available to contemporaries allowing such truths to be disregarded).[5] Embedded traits they had internally valorized or suffered as components of their subjective singularity had to be re-cognized in the wake of their encounter with Bourdieu as the products of recurrent social relations and regularities and their own obscurely conscious strategies within these. Bourdieu's sustained and rarely qualified assault on the presuppositions of a whole literary 'ethos' appeared to see in that ethos little worth endorsing or cultivating. He perhaps saw no strategic point in thus attenuating his critique.[6] The literary ethos as a kind of brute social fact was ingrained into the processes of secondary and higher education, and thereby into more general processes of social reproduction. Its exposure in these terms outweighed any concern to protect any of its elements.

Already in *Reproduction*, however, Bourdieu's own 'reductionist' critique is uncannily mirrored by a different kind of reductionist evacuation of literary concerns. He observes in a footnote that, following survey analysis,

beyond the manifestations of the old alliance between the dominant fractions of the bourgeoisie and those teachers most attached (...) to the traditional mode of recruitment and training, and by the same token, to the traditional conception of culture (the 'humanities'), one glimpses the first signs of a new alliance between those fractions of the dominant classes most directly tied to production and the management of the State apparatus and those categories of teachers capable of expressing their categorial interests (...) in the technocratic language of rationality and productivity. (*R*, 215)

These prodromes would, two decades later, become in a sense the key theme of *The State Nobility*, his account of the structural transformations of the field of higher education and elite-producing agencies in twentieth-century France. By that time, it was clear to Bourdieu that an economistic and productivist ethos and its associated rhetoric had become the dominant logic in this field. The symbol of this mutation was the now multiply attested dominance of the École Nationale d'Administration over the École Normale Supérieure in France's 'field of power'.[7] But there were other signs, not least the rise of lesser *grandes écoles* and private business schools promoting direct subservience to economic demands and an avowedly 'anti-academic' disposition to a student clientele that was already more than half-converted.[8] The overcrowded and underfunded humanities departments of French universities were little match for these. Bourdieu would note not just how the attractiveness of humanities degrees was being corroded, but how their very purpose was becoming increasingly unclear in general perception, with arts students appearing as socially 'useless'.[9] There were now powerfully institutionalized economic and political processes performing their own 'scouring' work on representations of literary education. As these very economic and political processes became the privileged object of Bourdieu's critical concern, his own representation of literature and its teachings became more expressly complex.

Canons, Critique and the Shadow of the Demi-habile

This is not to underplay the enduringly confrontational posture which Bourdieu would continue to adopt in relation to a certain 'universe' of literary studies construed as a whole (as he would, in other components of his œuvre, in relation to other institutional and discursive universes such as economics, philosophy, art history, linguistics, or public administration).[10] *The Rules of Art*, published in 1992, was widely perceived as, at worst, an all-out attack on approaches to literature in the academy, or, at best, a comprehensive endeavour to annex literary study under an all-embracing sociology. In it, Bourdieu frequently challenges a founding gesture that permits the teaching of literature as such: the selection of particular textual works and their integration into a canon for pedagogical transmission.

Bourdieu recurrently underlines the decontextualizing operation that this implies as an impediment to the 'true' understanding of the work in question:

Paradoxically, we can only be sure of some chance of participating in the author's subjective intention (. . .) provided we complete the long work of objectification necessary to reconstruct the universe of positions within which he was situated and where what he wanted to do was defined. (*RA*, 88)

Such formulae recur (here the absolute restriction ('can only . . . provided') is actually intensified by the concessionary 'some' — see also *RA*, 98). Indeed the contextualization Bourdieu advocates goes substantially beyond reconstructing what may consciously have been in the mind of the writer, as this can only be understood in terms of unexplicated socially structured logics bearing upon his mental operations, both in terms of the evolving specific artistic 'field' within which he is working, and the equally evolving and interlocking 'fields' that make up society as a whole at any given moment. One is tempted to evoke a 'hypercontextualizing' imperative at work in Bourdieu's theorized methodology (as I suggested above, this is not always quite the same thing as his real method). For not only must one reconstruct multiple 'spaces' or 'fields' within which the work in question takes on its 'differential value' or significance. One must also, Bourdieu writes, perform a 'double historicization' (*RA*, 309): readers must carry out a reflexive contextualization of their own position and trajectory in a 'field', and that field's position in a wider mutating social space, in order to reach a level of lucidity as to their appropriation of and investment in the particular enliteratured object in question.

Where will it, or can it, stop? Engagement in the labile magma of literature is inevitably mediated through readings of readings of readings. A chronologically ordered arithmetic succession of 'historicizations' is unlikely to capture much of the process's exponentialized errancy. Yet the principal objection to Bourdieu's 'hypercontextualizing' imperative need not be that its postulates are false. One can plausibly concede that the heave and slippage of literary magma are caught through and through in the gravitational pull of social force-fields. It seems preferable to demonstrate this, as Bourdieu does in several contexts, rather than leave literary indeterminacy as a night where all cows are black. And the standard objection of 'reductionism' seems itself rather reductive. It fails to do justice to the care Bourdieu takes not to fold, in this case, the literary onto the 'social' as a whole, but to construct the field of the literary as such, the field of literary position-takings as such, the mutating field of literary styles as such, and so on. One's principal objection to Bourdieu's thrust here can instead be formulated in pragmatic terms — both at the level of a day-to-day reading practice, and, to coin a term that might be an oxymoron in Bourdieu's lexis, at a 'scholastico-practical' level.[11]

One way of suggesting this (*cum grano salis*) is to anticipate what I will present below as Bourdieu's own real practice, and to tear from its original context a verbal fragment from Pascal's *Pensées* (formulated as an objection to Descartes), and see where it takes us in understanding differently where Bourdieu's argument is leading us:

In general terms one must say: 'That is the result of figure and motion,' because it is quite true, but to name them and assemble the machine is quite ridiculous. It is pointless, uncertain, and arduous [*pénible*]. Even if it were true we do not think that the whole of the philosophy would be worth an hour's effort.[12]

Who would ever pick up a new book if the 'only' way they had 'some' chance of understanding anything at all of what the author could show them was via the fastidious kinds of historicizing hypercontextualization described by Bourdieu? In admittedly excessive manner, Pascal's note indicates something of the calculus of attention that all interpretative strategies must negotiate. In the case at hand, one might say that an obsessive attention to a text's genesis (the 'machines' of its production and reception) may inhibit the perception of a text's potential (to unfold itself in different contexts). Bourdieu argues that his theorization of literature in *The Rules of Art* can 'intensify' the experience of ordinary reading (*RA*, xvii). That may be so, though it is hard to avoid thinking of a trope recurrently mobilized by Iain McGilchrist in his study of divided brain function: 'does placing a maths professor in a circus troupe result in a flying mathematician, or a bunch of trapeze artists who can no longer perform unless they have first calculated the precise trajectory of their leap?' (McGilchrist surmises that such 'anomalies' can lead to both 'unusual talents and unusual deficits').[13]

As a research strategy, Bourdieu's 'strong' version of field theory as applied to literature is a stimulating horizon for a particular kind of literary-historical and sociological comprehension.[14] As a pedagogical norm, it would appear at first sight to be unworkable. It is hard enough in most pedagogical situations to get pupils and students to pay sustained attention to a single text, let alone the multiplicity of contemporaneous texts alongside which it emerged, and against which alone its putatively original 'differential value' can be perceived. The issues emerge in some of their complexity — indeed perhaps more so than Bourdieu had anticipated when embarking on the paragraph — in the following passage from *Pascalian Meditations* (here in relation to analogous canonization processes at work in philosophy as well as the historical constitution of the Bible):

To combat this forgetting of history (. . .), I am tempted to set authority against superstition and to refer the devotees of hermeneutic philosophy, a strictly 'philosophical' reading of the texts consecrated by tradition as philosophical, to the various passages of the *Tractatus* in which Spinoza defines the programme for a genuine science of cultural works. Spinoza there invites the interpreters of the Books of the Prophets to break with the routine of hermeneutical exegeses and subject these works to a 'historical examination' seeking to determine not only 'the life, the conduct and the aim of the author of each book, who he was, what was the occasion, and the epoch of his writing, whom did he write for, and in what language,' but also 'into whose hands it fell... by whose advice it was received into the canon, and how the books now recognized as canonical were united into a single body.' This magnificently sacrilegious programme (...) contradicts point by point all the presuppositions of the liturgical reading, which, in a sense, is perhaps not as absurd as it might seem from the standpoint of a rather narrow reason, since it grants the canonical texts the false eternization of ritual embalming. (*PM*, 47–8; translation modified)

There is no doubting the interest of this Spinozist 'programme', for which Bourdieu's work provides an array of marvellous tools. But there are problems in setting it up as a kind of master paradigm for reading (facilitated in the passage above by the projection of an improbably 'pure' liturgical reading as Bourdieu's discursive foil). The final qualifying clause of the paragraph, appended like an afterthought, is revealing for our purposes. Having exposed the 'absurdity' of canons, predicated on 'abstraction' and the concomitant 'forgetting of history', it is as though Bourdieu concedes nonetheless something like their historical necessity. Admittedly, this is here rather in the mode of Durkheim conceding the necessity for the societies he studies of 'religions' as well-founded illusions (whatever their cognitive defects, they 'work' as mechanisms for protecting a society against entropic dispersal).[15] It is as though Bourdieu, reading over his argument, felt his own reasoning to be somewhat 'narrow'. Indeed, one senses here, as elsewhere in the *Pascalian Meditations*, the shadow of the *demi-habile*, Pascal's figure for the detached 'philosophical' critique of the absurdity of the world's ways that understands little of the necessities underlying those ways (see, for example, *P*, 90/83, 101/93). Bourdieu is happy to subsume others (or previous versions of himself) under the epithet (for example *PM*, 189–90), but the term has an uncanny capacity to transmute and re-emerge as a question mark over a new position (a feature of the unsettling Pascalian dynamic producing a 'continuous reversal' of perspective (*P*, 93/86; translation modified)). Bourdieu's reflection is vulnerable to the author under whose 'aegis' (*PM*, 1) he writes.

The pragmatic need which canons address need not be conceived as the 'false eternization of a ritual embalming'. Elsewhere in Bourdieu's work, we find elements of a practical resolution to the apparent antinomy presented above (between a thoroughgoing historicization of works and their integration into a transepochal canon with more than a purely historical interest). Bourdieu was asked on two occasions in the 1980s by socialist governments to head up commissions overseeing the recasting of school curricula. The transition from scouring sociologist exposing the 'arbitrariness' of all educational syllabuses and canons to an advisor outlining in normative mode the shape of a new syllabus was not straightforward for Bourdieu.[16] However, one move that figures prominently in his approach was the integration of the notion of 'cultural arbitrariness' itself as a core component of his proposed curricular guidelines.[17] If that really were to be made teachable, one might surmise that some kind of (meta-canonical) 'canon' might have to be specified — and one element in that might be a compendium of Spinozan fragments ripped from the *Tractatus* and re-organized for the purpose.

Pascal Out of Place

What Bourdieu actually does with literary resources throughout his œuvre is not reducible to the theory of literary fields as systematized in *The Rules of Art*. Curiously, however, the frames of that theory allow us to grasp something of his actual practice in the movement of its very divergence and *désinvolture* (as flying mathematician, perhaps, rather than inhibited trapeze artist). Jacques Dubois suggests that Bourdieu's posture in *The Rules of Art* as superpositioned explicator of Flaubert and his place in the nineteenth-century literary field does not correspond to the effective 'division of labour' that can be traced across his discussion. The text often reads instead rather like a cross-epochal 'collaboration': Flaubert sets challenges, raises objections, interjects, asks questions, offers advice for the sociologist's work elsewhere, and so on.[18] Similarly, Jérôme David, in a suggestive article, proposes that we distinguish in Bourdieu's writings between his emphatic self-positioning as a sociologist working 'on' literature, and his largely unthematized — and in some ways quite unusual — position as a sociologist 'in' literature.[19] To put it another way, Bourdieu is immersed not just in the protocols of sociology, but in a universe of literary and other cultural references. They comprise one compartment of the 'thinking tools' (discursive formulae, narrative techniques, 'takes' on aspects of the social world) that he has 'present' or to hand when confronting a given problem. His deployment of these tools often involves scant or no reference to the original fields of their production (his evocation of the 'paradigms' or 'effects', 'models' or 'limit-cases' proposed by such as Kafka or Cervantes involves an essentially 'internal' apprehension of their works (*PM*,

229, 160)). This opportunistic and creative appropriation, combining conceptual probing and rhetorical play with authorial authorities, does not invalidate Bourdieu's more self-consciously elaborated theory of literary production. It does allow us, however, to moderate 'from within' the annexionist or sometimes rather stifling claims that accompany the latter.

This practice of literarily available resources, their incorporation into the rhythms and reflexes of his thought, is perhaps nowhere so evident as in the *Pascalian Meditations*. The work carries a certain literary self-consciousness in its very framing: placing his reflections 'under the sign' or 'aegis' of Pascal certainly signals an affinity in conceptual preoccupations, as Bourdieu notes, and allows him to sidestep the usual affiliations in terms of which a sociologist might be expected to situate himself (Marx, Weber, Durkheim . . .).[20] But it also announces a certain affective tonality, underscored by the black cover of its original publication (contrasting on the shelf with the creamy white generally encasing Bourdieu's other publications). We expect certain leitmotifs: the vanity of human ends, and the vanity of denouncing distractions from that vanity; the finitude of thought in its bodily embedding; a measure of self-disgust in combination with apparently irrepressible movements of self-aggrandizement; the force of custom and servile 'imagination'; a sustained counterposing of the social animal's *misère* and *grandeur*. And that is indeed what we get. There is almost no engagement with the social or cultural fields in which Pascal's thought emerged. Such mention of these as we find operate in negatively permissive mode. Bourdieu argues that thinkers around Port-Royal, associated with the bourgeois aristocracy of the *robins*, may have been 'inclined' to critical dispositions with regard to the self-legitimizing claims of the traditional nobility, and to the temporal powers of Church and State (*PM*, 3, 157).[21] But this social interest in social lucidity does not, he says, 'invalidate the truths it uncovers' (3; translation modified). If Bourdieu is not quite 'eternalizing' those truths, he is crediting them with a decisive transhistorical potency, sufficient to unbind (or absolutize) them with regard to the site of their original formulation.

Yet Bourdieu does not simply derive from Pascal a series of abstract transposable propositions on the contingency of human engagement in social worlds. We find instead in the *Meditations* a sustained textual interleaving, indeed an insistent stylistic interpenetration. The purpose is certainly not to produce a 'commentary' on Pascal. Bourdieu rather enlists Pascal's crafted fragmentary artefacts — the semi-dispersed *pensées* of his *Nachlass* — as he circles around the themes that have driven his own œuvre, looking for ways of putting them into clearer, more acute or more arresting relief. Two extended quotations, selected from many, will give a sense of the conceptual and rhetorical play at work:

To find a way out of this interminable debate, one can simply start out from a paradoxical observation, condensed by Pascal into an admirable formula [*une très belle formule*], which immediately points beyond the dilemma of objectivism and subjectivism: 'By space the universe comprehends and swallows me up like an atom; by thought I comprehend the world.' The world encompasses me, comprehends me as a thing among things, but I, as a thing for which there are things, comprehend this world. And I do so (must it be added?) *because* it encompasses and comprehends me; it is through this material inclusion — often unnoticed or repressed — and what follows from it, the incorporation of social structures in the form of dispositional structures, of objective chances in the form of expectations or anticipations, that I acquire a practical knowledge and control of the encompassing space (. . .).

The reader will have understood that I have tacitly expanded the notion of space to include, as well as physical space, which Pascal is thinking of, what I call social space, the locus of the coexistence of social positions, mutually exclusive points, which, for the occupants, are the basis of points of view. (*PM*, 130; *P*, 113/104).[22]

Such might be the anthropological root of the ambiguity of symbolic capital — glory, honour, credit, reputation, fame — the principle of an egoistic quest for satisfactions of *amour propre* which is, at the same time, a fascinated pursuit of the approval of others: 'The greatest baseness of man is the pursuit of glory. But that is the greatest mark of his excellence; for whatever possessions he may have on earth, whatever health and essential comfort, he is not satisfied if he has not the esteem of men.' Symbolic capital enables forms of domination which implies dependence on those who can be dominated by it (. . .). (*PM*, 166; *P*, 470/435)

In the first quotation, the recourse to Pascal gives Bourdieu an abruptly authorized *entrée* into his subject that allows him to cut short a more conventionally philosophical discussion on the division of 'comprehensive' and 'explanatory' labour. The crystalline chiasmus of Pascal's fragment sends its expanding ripples into Bourdieu's amplificatory gloss and development. Its effects are both aesthetic and conceptual, as it becomes ingrained in the structures of Bourdieu's thought. The second passage works rather differently. The two discourses are held apart, each maintaining a relatively discrete lexis. The hinge is the colon, and one is reminded of Fowler's original definition of its function as being (in English) to '[deliver] the goods that have been invoiced in the preceding words'.[23] Pascal delivers the goods promised by Bourdieu's abstract concept of 'symbolic capital'. He brings it down to a certain existential ground. He can talk freely of man's 'baseness' or 'vileness', just as Bourdieu can 'use' him later to evoke directly the anthropological 'datum' of death and the refuge that 'we' as 'wretched and powerless fools' forlornly seek from this in 'society' (*PM*, 239; *P*, 151/141) (if Bourdieu were to invoke these terms in his own name, the ensuing 'naive' metaphysical pathos might tarnish his own scientific-symbolic capital). Just as Bourdieu admires in Kafka a certain 'brutality' of the imagination (see *PM*, 142) that he could not permit himself as a 'scientist', so he can use Pascal's uncompromising bluntness to underscore his more scholastic formulations. 'How can we not envy the freedom of writers?' he asks, only half-rhetorically, at the beginning of *Pascalian Meditations* (*PM*, 10; translation modified). His working solution appears to have been to integrate selected shards of that freedom into his own writing.

In a sense, Pascal anticipated such uses of his writing. He seems to have cultivated an art of writing that was an art of 'flighting' verbal fragments such that they would travel beyond the place where he crafted them and 'insinuate' their way not just into other writings, but into more ordinary verbal exchanges:

The style of Epictetus, Montaigne and Salomon de Tultie [an anagram of the pseudonym under which Pascal published his *Lettres provinciales*] is (. . .) the one which insinuates itself the most effectively, stays longest in the memory and is most often quoted, because it consists entirely of thoughts born from everyday conversations (. . .). (*P*, 745/628; translation modified)

Pascal thus anticipates and facilitates the fragmentary pragmatic redeployment of his *pensées* (a redeployment to which he himself had, of course, subjected in their turn authors such as those cited above). At the same time, the textual embrace to which Bourdieu subjects Pascal's writings also embodies a certain interpretative violence (while also, as Michael Moriarty notes, allowing us to see things in Pascal that otherwise would have remained undisclosed[24]). Admittedly, Bourdieu's intention is to bend Pascal's work to his purposes rather than provide a faithful account of that work. Nonetheless, by pointing up some aspects of the 'forcing' in question, we can not only avoid simply superimposing Bourdieu's 'science of man' upon Pascal's 'study of man'.[25] We can also bring into focus blind spots in Bourdieu's own thought.

Bourdieu's analysis of modern societies revolves around the genesis of 'fields' and 'sub-fields' through which they become internally differentiated, and which work as relatively autonomous domains each with their specific stakes, codes, laws of competition and forms of 'capital' (the legal field, the commercial field, the political field, the academic field, the journalistic field, the literary field, etc.). Perhaps unsurprisingly, he views the Pascalian scheme of 'orders' as an anticipation of his own distinctive field theory (*PM*, 15). The result is a certain folding of Pascal's scheme within the Bourdieusian frame of reference:

Each field, like the Pascalian 'order', thus involves its agents in its own stakes [*enjeux*], which, from another point of view, the point of view of another game, become invisible or at least insignificant or even illusory: 'All the glory of greatness [*grandeurs*] has no lustre for people who are in search of understanding [*dans les recherches de l'esprit*]. The greatness of clever men [*gens de l'esprit*] is invisible to kings, to the rich, to chiefs, and to all the worldly great. The greatness of wisdom (...) is invisible to the carnal-minded and to the clever. These are three orders differing in kind.' (*PM*, 97; *P*, 308/290)

Undeniably, an exposition of Pascal's scheme of incommensurable 'orders' provides a telling demonstration through defamiliarization of the principles underpinning Bourdieu's more general theory. In particular, Pascal brings into compelling relief the Bourdieusian concept of the *illusio* — the agent's prereflexive investment in the particular stakes (the *lusiones*) of the 'social game' that has invested him, and that may appear to agents otherwise invested as mere 'illusion'. Bourdieu sees in literature and the literary field areas where agents' relations to an *illusio* become particularly complex and thus revealing, due in part to the sustained and reflexive engagement with illusion qua illusion that is a necessary feature of participation in the field. Yet the Pascalian scheme, like other literary treatments one could name, does more than illustrate the Bourdieusian frame: it also stretches and challenges it.[26]

It may be that the Pascalian orders are more illuminatingly set athwart rather than within Bourdieusian fields. The 'order of the flesh' (or of worldly grandeurs) and the 'order of the mind' do not really correspond to discrete fields. The point may be made clearly if we map these two Pascalian terms onto their Augustinian correlates (that Bourdieu also uses elsewhere). The *libido sentiendi* and *libido dominandi* (broadly the 'order of the flesh' for Pascal) and the *libido sciendi* (the order of the mind) operate transversally across all fields in different combinations — both directly 'economic' fields and the kinds of economically 'anti-economic' fields represented in Bourdieu's analyses by the worlds of art, literature, science, and so on. At this level, the Pascalian terms give us a way of apprehending different modes of cathexis within the same field (Bourdieu approaches this in describing the attraction exerted by different 'poles' within a given field). However, the third of Pascal's orders (of 'charity' or 'wisdom') not only does not resemble a social field in Bourdieu's sense. On the contrary, it is constituted as the very antithesis of the principles that are deployed by Bourdieu to explain human behaviour across all social fields: the pursuit of imagined self-interest as prereflexively represented in specific forms of 'capital', recognition, or position. Pascal's 'order of charity' is organized around a set of vanishing points with regard to the logic of what he calls 'the world': 'God' as participation in 'universal being' whose value is not dependent on relative scarcity or position (*P*, 420/397); 'love' as a decentering of the self (597/509); an embrace of an 'obscurity' ('what the world calls obscurity' (300/282)) which Bourdieu tends to equate to 'social death'. Clearly, Pascal is writing of these dimensions of socio-affective life within the divided religious culture of his time. But they nonetheless represent a significant challenge to the frames of Bourdieu's analyses, and it is perhaps not surprising that the evocation of this 'order' is followed almost immediately by explicit 'digressions' in Bourdieu's analyses (*PM*, 97, 102). Bourdieu's engagement with a literature free to speak of many unscientific things leaves behind an instructive residue.[27]

Bourdieu can often give the impression that any teachings which literature has to offer need the intervention of a social 'science' if they are to be apprehended in their full truth. We saw how the teaching of literature was instructive for the sociologist essentially because it raised to a paradigmatic level the mystifications inherent in the pedagogical relation. Similarly, what Flaubert could teach us about his social world needed to be 'uncovered' and 'explicated' by the sociologist (putting to one side the disjuncture between this manifest theory and the nature of the real 'collaboration' between Flaubert and Bourdieu). Bourdieu would increasingly grant in his later work that literary resources could variously help social scientific work. But it may be that those resources also have teachings that cannot be so readily integrated into the *illusio* of the scientific disposition. In *Reproduction*, Bourdieu includes as an epithet to chapter two of book two the famous *pensée* in which Pascal evokes the 'red robes' and the 'ermine' of magistrates, the 'cassocks' and 'mules' of contemporary medics, the 'over-ample robes' of academics as apparels designed to distract from the vulnerability of their knowledge and inspire respect. Strangely,

Bourdieu elides from the passage, without marking his elision, Pascal's reference to the 'vain instruments' of 'imaginary sciences' designed to strike blows to people's 'imagination' and 'attract respect' (see *R*, 107 and *P*, 44/41).[28] Bourdieu appears scrupulous elsewhere in that book in marking elisions — what are we to make of this apparent 'avoidance of compromising formulations' (*R*, 125)? Was there a fear, perhaps, that Pascal's formulae might lead readers to recognize in Bourdieu's rhetoric certain traits that he did not want recognized as such? Some of the 'free writings' collected as 'literature' may carry teachings that elude an epoch's scientific policing.

NOTES

1 Pierre Bourdieu and Jean-Claude Passeron, *The Inheritors: French Students and their Relation to Culture* [1964], translated by Richard Nice (Chicago: University of Chicago Press, 1979), hereafter referred to as *I*; *Reproduction in Education, Society and Culture* [1970], translated by Richard Nice (London: Sage, 1990), hereafter *R*; Emile Durkheim, *The Evolution of Educational Thought: Lectures on the Formation and Development of Secondary Education in France*, translated by Peter Collins (London: Routledge, 1977), original French lectures 1905. I am very grateful to Michael Moriarty for his comments on an earlier draft of this article.

2 See for example Bourdieu, *Homo Academicus* [1984], translated by Peter Collier (Cambridge: Polity Press, 1988). On the 'conflict of faculties' as originally analysed by Kant, and the place of social science in more recent stagings of the question, see Alain Renaut, *Les Révolutions de l'université: essai sur la modernisation de la culture* (Paris: Calmann-Lévy, 1995), 138–46.

3 See for example Bourdieu, *The Rules of Art: Genesis and Structure of the Literary Field* [1992], translated by Susan Emanuel (Cambridge: Polity, 1996), hereafter *RA*, 32–4; *Pascalian Meditations* [1997], translated by Richard Nice (Cambridge: Polity, 2000), hereafter *PM*, 229.

4 Bourdieu, *Les Héritiers, les étudiants et leur culture* (Paris: Minuit, 1985), 88 (from a footnote not included in the English translation).

5 Annie Ernaux, 'Bourdieu, le chagrin', *Le Monde*, 6 February 2002; and Hélène Merlin-Kajman, 'Ne... que ou l'impossible traque des vanités', in *Bourdieu et la littérature*, edited by Jean-Pierre Martin (Nantes: Cécile Defaut, 2010), 155–72 (156). Interestingly, in light of my discussion below, Merlin-Kajman suggests that what prevented her developing like others a full-blown devotion to Bourdieusian 'scientism' as a result of this experience was her concomitant work on French seventeenth-century moralists, which

confronted her with analogous experiences of disruptive 'recognition' mediated through literary form.

6　Occasional qualifications such as the following are nonetheless important: 'it is not sufficient to observe that academic culture is a class culture; to proceed as if it were *only* that, is to help it remain so' (*I*, 72; translation modified).

7　See for example Pierre Bourdieu, *The State Nobility: Elite Schools in the Field of Power* [1988], translated by Lauretta Clough (Cambridge: Polity, 1996), 213–14.

8　Bourdieu, *State Nobility*, 224.

9　Bourdieu, 'A Refusal to be Cannon-fodder for the Bosses' [1986], in Bourdieu, *Political Interventions: Social Science and Political Action* [2002], edited by Franck Poupeau and Thierry Discepolo, translated by David Fernbach (London: Verso, 2008), 167–72 (170).

10　Bourdieu's abiding agenda was to show how the presuppositions of such discourses carry but mask certain social logics that a 'critical sociology' can disclose.

11　Bourdieu, in his simultaneous construction and critique of 'scholastic' logic, tends to oppose it to 'practical logic' (*PM*, passim). For a sympathetic critique, see Pierre Macherey, 'Bourdieu critique de la raison scolastique: le cas de la lecture littéraire', in *Bourdieu et la littérature*, edited by Martin, 113–41. My argument at this point is also indebted to Oliver Davis's discussion of the notions of overcontextualization, anachronism and literarity in the work of Jacques Rancière (see Davis, *Jacques Rancière* (Cambridge: Polity Press, 2010), 67–72, 107–15).

12　Blaise Pascal, *Pensées*, translated by A. J. Krailsheimer (London: Penguin, 1995), hereafter *P*. Krailsheimer uses the Lafuma numbering for the fragments. References will give this numbering, and then the numbering of the more recent French edition, Blaise Pascal, *Pensées*, edited by Michel Le Guern (Paris: Gallimard, 2004); in this case 84/77 (translation modified).

13　Iain McGilchrist, *The Master and His Emissary: The Divided Brain and the Making of the Western World* (New Haven: Yale University Press, 2009), 12–13.

14　See Jacques Dubois, 'Flaubert analyste de Bourdieu', in *Bourdieu et la littérature*, edited by Martin, 77–91 (77) and, in the present special issue, the articles by Anna Boschetti, Gisèle Sapiro and Michel Hockx.

15　See for example Durkheim, *The Elementary Forms of the Religious Life* [1912], translated by Joseph Ward Swain (London: George Allen, 1976), 2–3.

16　On these commissions, see Jeremy Ahearne, *Intellectuals, Culture and Public Policy in France: Approaches from the Left* (Liverpool: University of Liverpool Press, 2010), 138–50.

17　See *Propositions pour l'enseignement de l'avenir élaborées à la demande de Monsieur le Président de la République par les professeurs du Collège de France* (Paris: Collège de France, 1985), 14.

18 Dubois, 'Flaubert analyste de Bourdieu', 85.

19 Jérôme David, 'Sur un texte énigmatique de Pierre Bourdieu', *A contrario*
    4:2 (2006), 71–84 (76), translated for this volume by John Speller as 'On an
    Enigmatic Text by Pierre Bourdieu'.

20 See the original French cover blurb, as well as *PM*, 1.

21 Compare the classic work of Lucien Goldmann, *The Hidden God: A Study of
    Tragic Vision in the Pensées of Pascal and the Tragedies of Racine* [1955], translated
    by Philip Thody (London: Routledge, 1964). To an extent that his external
    (non-sociologist) critics seldom acknowledge, Bourdieu takes considerable
    care to avoid the typical 'reductions' commonly associated with sociological
    explanation.

22 Bourdieu and the English translation refer to the older 'Brunschvicg' edition,
    not now generally used. For convenience I have indicated where the requisite
    fragments can be found in the editions indicated above.

23 H. W. Fowler, *A Dictionary of Modern English Usage* [1926] (Oxford: Oxford
    University Press, 1961), under the heading 'Stops'.

24 Michael Moriarty, *Early Modern French Thought: The Age of Suspicion* (Oxford:
    Oxford University Press, 2003), 107.

25 For Bourdieu's term, see the cover blurb to the original French edition of
    PM; for Pascal's term see *P*, 687/581.

26 Bourdieu sees in the literary figure of the adolescent or youth, not yet
    definitively invested in any of the social games that are already partially
    investing him, as a revealing device, particularly in the hands of a novelist
    like Flaubert, for bringing into focus the logic of social games as such (*RA*,
    12–13). One might cite also the converse device, deployed for example in the
    late novels of Philip Roth, of virtuoso players of specific social games who are
    displaced from those games through a combination of 'accidentally' contrived
    social disgrace and/or biological decay, thereby bringing the *illusio* at the
    heart of those games into startling relief (for example in *American Pastoral*, *The
    Human Stain*, *Exit Ghost* or *The Humbling*).

27 It is possible to see the order of charity as being treated in different
    ways by Pascal in two of the key fragments in which the concept
    of orders is developed. At *P*, 58/54, an order of the 'pious' seems
    to operate on the same level and homologously to orders of the
    'strong', the 'beautiful' and the 'clever', even if the specific principles
    informing these orders are incommensurable (they do indeed function
    rather like discrete Bourdieusian fields). At *P*, 308/290, however, this
    incommensurability is, as it were, exponentialized: emphasis is laid on
    the 'infinite distance' between the grandeurs of the physical world
    and those of the mind, which itself functions as a figure of an
    'infinitely more infinite distance' between these and the principles of 'true
    charity' (which thereby challenge the functioning of the world's orders).

I am indebted to Michael Moriarty for suggesting this distinction. The space between these two treatments can be compared, *mutatis mutandis*, to the space in contemporary thought mapped out across differently construed economies and anti-economies of the gift (such as are found in the work of Bourdieu himself, Derrida or de Certeau).

28   The elision of the elision is carried into the English translation. Some three decades later, Bourdieu quotes in extended fragmented form the same extract at *PM*, 171, but closes the citation at the point where the references to science as display begin.

On an Enigmatic Text by Pierre Bourdieu

Jérôme David

Abstract:

A largely unknown commentary by Pierre Bourdieu on the poet Guillaume Apollinaire allows us to explore the non-theoretical, and even non-theorized, aspects of the relationship between the sociologist and literature. The present article begins by analysing Bourdieu's 1995 text as an example of close reading or *explication de texte* emerging, as it were, from a 'scholastic unconscious' dating from the 1950s. The article then proceeds to look at other ways in which Bourdieu has had recourse to literary references in his work (as a repertoire of techniques, as rhetorical elements for an argument from authority, as an equivalent or approach to sociological analysis, as ethical models or invocations). The article argues that, over and beyond his sociological objectification of literature, Bourdieu entertained a range of other relations to literature. These cannot be subsumed under a single theoretical system, but emerge at different times and with different, sometimes apparently 'anachronistic', effects.

Keywords: literature, sociology, Pierre Bourdieu, Apollinaire

'It goes without saying that we are right to expect—and that I expect—from literature much more than the revelation of the "real".' (Pierre Bourdieu)[1]

Among the innumerable texts that Pierre Bourdieu devoted to literature, a short four-page article, in my opinion, deserves particular attention. It is not a synthetic formulation of his sociology of fields, nor even an analysis that exemplifies his method. Published in 1995, the

Jérôme David's article was published in French as 'Sur un texte énigmatique de Pierre Bourdieu', *A Contrario* 4:2 (2006), 71–84. It has been translated by John Speller, and is reproduced by kind permission of its author and original publisher.

Paragraph 35.1 (2012): 115–130
DOI: 10.3366/para.2012.0045
© Edinburgh University Press
www.eupjournals.com/para

article in question is a commentary on a poem by Apollinaire entitled 'Automne malade' ('Autumn Ill'), and included in *Alcools* (1912).[2] It appears in the *Bibliographie des travaux de Pierre Bourdieu,* compiled by Yvette Desault and Marie-Christine Rivière,[3] but it has never for all that been mentioned by sociologists of literature.[4]

This invisibility is not in itself surprising, when one considers that Bourdieu's œuvre comprises several hundred titles. From this point of view, 'Apollinaire, Automne malade' simply shares the fate of several other rarely cited texts.[5] What makes these four pages so unique, and so disorienting for a reader familiar with the sociologist's work, is something else. One could speak of a shift in perspective from his usual analysis, or of a break in tone. But then one would forget that the article mobilizes notions developed elsewhere in his œuvre, and that it is therefore, on certain points, very much in conformity with what one might expect from a text signed by Bourdieu.

What is it, then? That is what I will try to clarify here, beginning with the feeling of perplexity that struck me on the first reading, and because the effort to make sense of this initial surprise has led me to read Bourdieu differently from how I had read him before, and differently perhaps from how he himself wished to be read. In fact, these four pages invite a reflection on the range of different relations, scholarly or otherwise, which the author held with literature over the course of his career; and they call for a very particular interpretative effort, which consists in breaking with a strictly intellectual approach to his sociology.

Logical Development and Affective Development

Bourdieu's argument follows the linear progression of stanzas in the poem. A complete transcription of Apollinaire's text opens the analysis, after which the commentary merges with a gloss proceeding verse by verse, and divided into four main parts. The first part develops, to take up a term that is subsequently deployed (133/331), the 'theme' of the first stanza:

'Autumn ill and adored', autumn adored *because of* its illness, because of its mortality. Is not Apollinaire, the poet of the flux of time, of the death of love, also the poet of the love of death, of the love of the passing of time, of the love of love as the terrain *par excellence* of this frailty? (131–2/330)

Two paragraphs follow which amplify this idea, by identifying the 'antitheses' set up by Apollinaire between the wind and roses, or the snow and orchard.

The second part, entitled 'The exhortation to *amor fati*', paraphrases the three following verses of the poem, including some very general allusions to the historical context (*'fin de siècle* spirit', *'fin de siècle* spleen'), and a reference to *Pelléas et Mélisande* by Debussy, whose name had already been evoked in the commentary on the first stanza. At this point, midway through the article, the reader cannot help but be surprised that Bourdieu does not change the register, but stays in the mode of literary close reading:

The poet speaks of *fatum*, but also proffers an exhortation to *amor fati*. (…) He gives autumn a lesson in philosophy, which consists, simply, of drawing a lesson in philosophy that is already inscribed in autumn. Die. Accept your destiny, which is to die. *Ama fatum*. But to accept one's destiny is, for autumn, to *die in beauty*, which is to say 'to die in whiteness and richness', two words which, by their alliance, remind us of the preceding stanza, which is to say of the snow, a sumptuous shroud in the orchard, a menaced abundance. But the antithesis becomes a synthesis: the mortal snow and the richness of ripe fruits are reconciled in the *fatal beauty* of a luxurious decadence, so profoundly in harmony with the *fin de siècle* spirit. (132/331)

'The Fatal Instant', the third part of the analysis, enriches the reading of Apollinaire with a quotation from a poem by Verlaine put to music by Debussy, which, following the example of certain lines of 'Autumn Ill', according to Bourdieu, consists of a 'song which announces death' (133/331).

The final part, 'Resignation', is the longest. We find Debussy, for the melancholy of his *Préludes* and *Mélodies*, next to Turner and the 'Impressionist painters', summoned for their part because of their attention to the 'most fleeting details' (134/332). The paraphrase is also enriched by quotations drawn from other poems in *Alcools* ('Sur le pont Mirabeau' (The Mirabeau Bridge), 'L'adieu' (The Farewell), 'L'automne' (Autumn), 'Marie' and 'Cors de Chasse' (Hunting Horns)), as well as a reference to 'Les Djinns' by Hugo, and another to Schopenhauer. The focus remains on the variation of poetic themes:

The poet declares himself: he speaks in the first person ('And how I love') and to declare his love to autumn (the culmination of the whole logical and affective movement of the poem). (…) 'Autumn ill and adored': the poet loves autumn because of its illness. What he loves in autumn is the death of autumn, just as he loves in love the death of love; his love of love is a love of death. (133/332)

Having reached the end of the article, however, we are left waiting for the *sociologist* to declare himself. For if a notion such as *amor fati*, for example, is often evoked by Bourdieu to explain the effect of self-evidence born of the conformity between a habitus and the social world of which it is the product,[6] it is not discussed on the same level in this article: *amor fati* does not have here the status of an analytical category, but of a philosophical theme inherited from Schopenhauer and taken up by Apollinaire; it is a feature of the object for commentary, a facet of the 'lesson in philosophy' exemplified by the poem, and not a theoretical term injected by the commentator. The possible link that the reader might draw between this exegetical use of the notion and the descriptive use Bourdieu reserves for it in other texts, between the paraphrastic *amplificatio* of a stanza and the rigorous characterization of certain social facts, rests on an approximate synonymy, or better, on an operation that the 1995 article does not carry out but leaves its reader to perform. For *amor fati*, because it belongs to Bourdieu's standard lexicon — it is a frequent entry in the indexes to his works — induces a feeling of familiarity in the reader, an involuntary memory. But this spontaneous recognition, by overdetermining our understanding of what exactly the notion means in this commentary on Apollinaire, tends, in my view, to substitute a logical sense, extrapolated from Bourdieu's works in sociology or anthropology, for this other sense which interests me, but which proves very difficult to qualify — except by returning, provisionally, to the distinction advanced in the commentary between the *logical* movement and *affective* movement of a text. In a way, one must go against the theoretical systematicity of Bourdieu's œuvre, which is at once so self-evident and so repeatedly asserted, to be able to see that we might not be dealing here with theory, nor even, perhaps, with science, but with an affective attachment to certain literary works, and to a certain mode of reading them.[7]

Socio-historical contextualization requires analogous treatment. If one is familiar with the theory of fields, or with the lectures at the Collège de France devoted to Manet, one might be tempted to imagine what Bourdieu could have wished to *imply* by 'the literary circles of the time' (134/333), or by the references to Turner, the impressionists, or to Debussy (if one also supposes that the hypothesis of a homology between different artistic fields, which he seemed to elaborate more and more minutely, would have opened the way to a rigorous sociology of intermediality). In his analysis of the poem by Apollinaire, however, Bourdieu does not even begin to imply that he is doing sociology, or that he might go on to do sociology. What he gives us, in this 1995 article, is an *explication de texte*. No more, no less: this is not sociology of literature, in the sense that he gave this term in *The Rules of Art*,[8] for example, but nor is it an exegesis devoid of panache. This last statement renders even more complex the status of this text: the sociologist, scourge of literary reading,[9] submits to the rigours of a scholastic exercise, in which he succeeds rather well, and whose pedagogical purpose is, in general, to familiarize students with the conditions of a canonical reading.[10] In other words, this analysis would not stand up to the trivial test of logical coherence, if one subjected it to the test of its author's sociology, since the latter associates the very principle of literary commentary with a collective form of *scholastic fallacy*.

Once again, then, our understanding of these pages clashes with the criteria of academic interpretation. For such interpretation hinders our reading of the article in itself: either because it encourages us to approach it as a repetition of what the sociologist has said elsewhere, in more rigorous fashion, or because it leads us to view it only as a contradiction of the presuppositions contained in his sociological thinking, which we can therefore justifiably either ignore or put down to extrinsic and contingent factors, such as the circumstances of its publication.[11]

There are, however, at least two ways out of this formidable aporia. The first requires us to characterize very precisely the type of scholastic exercise that Bourdieu is undertaking, so that we can date its presuppositions. It then appears, as I will argue in the conclusion, that a long-buried *scholastic unconscious* reveals itself in the article on Apollinaire, which the sociologist does not deem it necessary to restrain, insofar as, being the precursor of the *la nouvelle critique* (new criticism) which he made the initially tacit, then declared, rival of his sociology of literature, this approach to works does not appear suspect to him. Indeed, it appeared all the less suspect since, by 1995, *la nouvelle critique* no longer presented the united intellectual front, nor the conceptual coherence which had made it such a threat to a sociologist working on Flaubert, provoking a denunciation that extended, indirectly, to any 'internal' reading of works. According to such a hypothesis, this exegesis of Apollinaire would not contradict the sociological reflections of Bourdieu, because it is partly separate from them.

The second escape route involves reading between the concepts, so to speak. Instead of looking for a way to link this almost incongruous text to one or another of the intellectual position-takings of its author, one might try to glimpse at work here a non-theoretical, and even un-theorized, relation to literature. We can then ask in what modes this *literary* imagination is deployed, and with what consequences for his sociology. And this question requires us to read Bourdieu less as a sociologist *of* literature, and more as a sociologist *in* literature.

A Sociologist in Literature

References to certain literary works seem to have stimulated Bourdieu's academic thought. We find them in most of his texts, in the form of analytical arguments, citations, epigraphs or allusions, even when the subject does not generally involve literature. In this sense, the sociologist most frequently uses literature not to put forward his sociology, but to prepare or support, or even fill in the gaps in its reasoning. It is therefore important to distinguish Bourdieu's sociological relation to literature, which does not really interest me here, and this other nexus of relations of collusion and alliance he maintained with literary writers.

Without going into details that would take us well beyond the limits of a journal article, I would like to identify four modalities of this non-objectifying relation of Bourdieu to literature: (a) the recourse to literary works envisaged as a repertoire of techniques (enunciative, narrative or stylistic) which can be transferred to sociological writing; (b) the invocation of canonical authors in support of sociological arguments that might not otherwise be accepted by cultivated readers (an argument from authority); (c) the reference to a literary text presented as a more or less rigorous equivalent of sociological analysis; (d) the explication of the literary ethic of a writer as a detour to evoke the academic or personal ethic of the sociologist. In each case, Bourdieu mobilizes literature for its *technical*, *rhetorical*, *analytical* and *ethical* resources. The differentiation of these uses provides only a glimpse of the multiple possible levels of entanglement between literature and the social sciences, and should be accompanied by a consideration of how these relations to works mesh within sociological texts. I will restrict myself, however, to illustrating these four points with the help of some significant examples, which is to say without discussing or comparing all the occurrences of literature I have noted in Bourdieu's works.

(a) It is no doubt in *Invitation to a Reflexive Sociology* that one finds the most explicit formulation of the *technical* reference to literature:

> The linear life-stories with which ethnographers and sociologists are content are artificial and (...) the apparently exceedingly formal researches of Virginia Woolf, Faulkner, or Claude Simon (...) appear today to me to be more 'realistic' (if the word has any meaning), anthropologically more truthful, closer to the truth of temporal experience, than the linear narratives to which traditional novels have accustomed us.
>
> Thus I was led to bring back to the fore of my thinking a whole set of questions that had been repressed concerning biography and, more generally, on the logic of the interview as a process, i.e., on the relations between the temporal structure of lived experience and the structure of discourse and, at the same time, to raise to the status of legitimate scientific discourse, worthy of scientific publication and debate, a whole range of so-called 'raw' documents that I tended to exclude, more unconsciously than consciously. In the same fashion, in my work on Flaubert, I stumbled upon many problems — and solutions — that he had himself encountered, such as that of the combined use of direct style, indirect style, and free indirect style which lies at the heart of the problem of transcription and publication of interviews.
>
> In short, I believe that literature, against which a good many sociologists have, from the origins to this day, thought necessary to define themselves in order to assert the scientificity of their discipline (...), is on many points more advanced than social science, and contains a whole trove of fundamental problems — those concerning the theory of narrative for instance — that sociologists should make their own and subject to critical examination instead of ostentatiously distancing themselves from forms of expression and thinking that they deem compromising.[12]

One might suppose that the genre of the interview, to which *An Invitation to Reflexive Sociology* belongs, would have incited the sociologist to divulge certain reflections on his work that these works themselves were not designed to explicate. But that would be to forget that the reflexivity claimed by Bourdieu has as its subject the epistemological operations of sociology and that it is characterized by their control *in* and *by* academic writing. We should not be surprised, then, to find in *Homo Academicus* an analogous passage:

> Thus it suffices to constitute as subject of a sentence the name of one of those collectivities fashionable in politics, to constitute the designated 'realities' as historical subjects able to posit and realize their own ends ('the People want...'). The objective teleology implied by this social anthropomorphism

coexists quite happily with a sort of spontaneous individualism, which is also inherent in the *subject-oriented* sentences of ordinary language, which, as in a fictional narrative, incline us to see the individual or collective history as a logical sequence of decisive actions. The sociologist thus finds himself faced with a writing problem very similar to that faced by novelists like Victor Hugo, especially in *Seventeen Ninety-Three*, and above all like Flaubert, when they wished to break with the privileged viewpoint of the 'hero' (...).[13]

For Bourdieu, then, these are 'writing problems' touching on narrative or enunciation, which writers had faced before sociologists had, and to which literary works could offer possible solutions.

(b) The rhetoric of the argument from authority is obvious in *Masculine Domination*, where the author draws explicitly on the recognized legitimacy of Virginia Woolf in the eyes of the majority of feminist intellectuals:

> It took all the insight of Virginia Woolf and the infinite refinement of her writing to pursue the analysis into the best-concealed effects of a form of domination which is inscribed in the whole social order and operates in the obscurity of bodies, which are both the stakes and the principles of its efficacy. And perhaps it was also necessary to invoke the authority of the author of *A Room of One's Own* to lend some credibility to the recalling of the hidden constants of the relation of sexual domination — so strong are the factors which, beyond simple blindness, incline people to ignore those constants (such as the legitimate pride of a feminist movement that is led to stress the advances won by its struggles).[14]

This use of a writer chosen in part for her social recognition, problematized as such in this passage, also sheds new light in return on the status of innumerable formulas that Bourdieu puts into his texts. Quotations from Cervantes, Claudel, Gide, Proust, Rilke or Virginia Woolf embellish such different texts as *Distinction*, *The Logic of Sense*, *Homo Academicus*, or *Pascalian Meditations*. They are presented most frequently as felicitous formulations expressing what sociology seeks to explain:

> As Claudel put it, 'connaître, c'est naître avec', to know is to be born with, and the long dialectical process, often described as 'vocation', through which the various fields provide themselves with agents equipped with the *habitus* needed to make them work, is to the learning of a game very much as the acquisition of the mother tongue is to the learning of a foreign language.[15]

Or, more surprisingly:

> What is acquired in daily contact with ancient objects, by regular visits to antique-dealers and galleries, or, more simply, by moving in a universe of familiar, intimate objects 'which are there', as Rilke says, 'guileless, good, simple, certain', is of course a certain 'taste', which is nothing other than a relation of immediate familiarity with the things of taste. But it is also the sense of belonging to a more polished, more polite, better policed world, a world which is justified in existing by its perfection, its harmony and beauty, a world which has produced Beethoven and Mozart and continues to produce people capable of playing and appreciating them. And finally it is an immediate adherence, at the deepest level of the habitus, to the tastes and distastes, sympathies and aversions, fantasies and phobias which, more than declared opinions, forge the unconscious unity of a class.[16]

These formulas function in the mode of the argument from authority on two levels: they draw on the cultural baggage of the reader, and on the 'seriousness' they accord to the works mentioned, so that the sociology that arrives at the same conclusions is surreptitiously validated; they signal to the reader that the sociology of taste is not the work of a sociologist without it, since he shares their literary knowledge. This is the reason, despite the fact that these formulas frequently involve more than this rhetorical use of literature, specifically in providing an intuitive grasp of the social world that Bourdieu sets himself the task of elaborating (this is the next point), that I have thought it necessary to deal with this point separately.

(c) Literary works provide Bourdieu with a sort of bottomless collection of insights into the social world, whose variable degree of veracity sometimes attains the status of sociological truth. The recourse to literature produces in his view knowledge effects whose importance for academic reasoning depends on the degree of explication and coherence which writers have given to their intuitions of certain social phenomena. The descriptive or theoretical value of literary texts could thus be measured by their specific dosage of sociography and sociology, to use the distinction made by Jean-Claude Passeron,[17] which is to say of literary or ordinary common sense and of reflexive consideration of the prejudices of their author and their readers. The knowledge imparted by literature therefore ranges, if one keeps to the terms used by Bourdieu, from the more or less successful 'evocation' of sociological 'principles' (Borges, Perec or Zola) to the 'model' or 'exemplary image' (*The Trial* by Kafka), a sort of polar case exemplifying the ideal-type of a social configuration, passing through the intermediary stages of 'incomparably lucid evocation' (Woolf) and of 'extreme lucidity' (La Rochefoucauld).[18] Proust, a little more than Kafka or Woolf,[19] seems to be the writer Bourdieu appreciates the most for the keenness of his perception of the social world. In fact, in his case novelistic evocation not only corroborates the conclusions of sociological research, and goes further even than expressing them more adequately than academic writing:

The statistics of the class distribution of newspaper reading would perhaps be interpreted less blindly if sociologists bore in mind Proust's analysis of 'that abominable, voluptuous act called "reading the paper", whereby all the misfortunes and cataclysms suffered by the universe in the last twenty-four hours — battles which have cost the lives of fifty thousand men, murders, strikes, bankruptcies, fires, poisonings, suicides, divorces, the cruel emotions of statesman and actor, transmuted into a morning feast for our personal entertainment, make an excellent and particularly bracing accompaniment to a few mouthfuls of *café au lait*.'[20] This description of the aesthete's variant invites an analysis of the class variations and the invariants of the mediated, relatively abstract experience of the social world supplied by newspaper reading, for example, as a function of variations in social and spatial distance (with, at one extreme, the local items in the regional dailies — marriages, deaths, accidents — and, at the other extreme, international news, or, on another scale, the royal engagements and weddings in the glossy magazines) or in political commitment (from the detachment depicted in Proust's text to the activist's outrage or enthusiasm).[21]

Literature goes so far, therefore, as to 'invite' the sociologist to specify his hypotheses, to refine the categories of his inquiry and to reinterpret the empirical data that has been collected, or the observations that have been made. It indicates what the sociologist should retain as pertinent phenomena. We are a long way from the subordination of literary works to the procedures of scientific objectification. And we must consider whether literature or, more precisely, the literary imagination of a sociologist might not develop, from being simply an invitation to research, to become an invitation to a social reverie — in other words, a formidable *epistemological obstacle*.[22]

(d) The *ethical* relation of Bourdieu to literature is perhaps the least obvious. It is nevertheless fully expressed in an article devoted to Ponge:

If one looks closely, one can understand and express the necessity of even the most different, the most foreign man: indeed not only a foreign man (facilitated, in this case, by ethnology, because of the absence of antagonistic interests) but a competing, hostile man (for example, the university, intimate friends and enemies). Absorbing oneself in the object in order to absorb it; at the extreme, identifying oneself with what one hates: this comprehension does not imply empathy at all, but a sort of intellectual pleasure (*amor intellectualis*), which is very close to the aesthetic pleasure of conforming to the law of the work; it comes from a sharp sense of the necessity bringing a man, if not to exist, then at least to exist as he is. This generative formula can be individual (Flaubert, Ponge) or generic (an aristocrat, a petit-bourgeois, a baker). (...) This intimate knowledge, which goes from the exterior to the interior, from the construction of the poet to the construction of the poem, is an arm against the object (...) but also against the subject of knowledge.

(...) Render the stranger necessary. One cannot be more of a humanist.[23]

Literature, because it is a form of knowledge, engages a diverse range of manners of knowing; and the critical commentary which renders them explicit opens the way to a reflection that Bourdieu himself qualifies as *ethical*:

Therefore I think that there is indeed (...) an ethical usage of reflexive sociology. Its purpose is not to 'pick' on others, to reduce them, to accuse them, to castigate them for, say, being 'the son of a mere so-and-so'. Quite the contrary. Reflexive sociology allows us to understand, to account for the world, or, to use an expression of Francis Ponge that I like a lot, to *necessitate the world* (...). This does not mean it has to be loved or preserved as it is.[24]

The Heterogenous Temporalities of a Thought

These different relations to literature, I have suggested, are not necessarily linked. And it happens that the discovery of a writer or the reading of a critic, or indeed the anniversary of the birth or death of a writer with its editorial effervescence, leads Bourdieu to adopt one or another of them.[25] The logic of each of these registers rarely being made explicit, and their coordination even more rarely being a specific object for reflection, it is possible to conceive of the interrelations between literature and sociology in Bourdieu's work as a sort of mobile composite of elements largely independent from each other, and each subject to its own particular oscillations. Nothing guarantees that the sociology of literature itself can regulate the general balance of these relations, nor that the arborescences I have indicated are insignificant in the movement as a whole.

Such an image enables us to conceptualize, by analogy with the reflection of certain historians concerning historical time,[26] a form of *anachronism* in Bourdieu's thought. This is not the chronological paralogism of a misfit between the epoch being studied and the categories of analysis, since this would suppose that Bourdieu's research was tied to a particular historical period, to which his sociological generalizations must be limited, which is not generally the case. Instead, it is the coexistence, over the course of a long period of individual research (a fortiori when it is punctuated by collective research), of heterogeneous temporalities that the present of an article or a book — which is to say the effort to apprehend *in one piece*, with a view to a single publication, all the pertinent aspects of a phenomenon — will never be able to absorb completely.

In this respect, the date 1995, when the article on Apollinaire was published, cannot necessarily be integrated into the linear history that one normally applies to scholarly or literary works. Perhaps it is not an element in a series whose preceding moment, in Bourdieu's work, would be *The Rules of Art* (1992), since the close reading of 'Automne malade' does not correspond to the strict temporality of the *theoretical* reflections of its author. The 1995 article derives, in my view, from Bourdieu's *ethical* relation to literature, and this relation does not have the same *tempo* as that of his sociological theory. Moreover, the dominant *ethic* justifies the relative indifference of the sociologist towards his own epistemological principles.

What is revealed in 'Apollinaire, Automne malade' is the scholastic unconscious of a largely dehistoricized relation to literature, indissociable from notions such as 'theme' or 'thesis' (anti- or syn-), which *la nouvelle critique* did its best to denounce from the 1960s, on the grounds that they assimilated literariness to the expression of a subjective consciousness or a message. In 1995, then, Bourdieu adopted a mode of reading dating from the 1950s in his analysis of Apollinaire, a mode of reading anterior to the 'structuralist *aggiornamento*' of *explications de texte*. And it may be argued that he felt able to write such a text for the very reason that he believed that he had delivered a fatal blow to *la nouvelle critique* in *The Rules of Art*, and that, having done his best to render theoretically null and void the dichotomy between 'internal' or formalist reading and 'external' or contextualized reading, he could not, almost on principle, be suspected of entertaining a 'naive' relation with texts.

'Each time unique'

The points made so far are not enough to solve the enigma of this anachronistic text from 1995. They have, however, discreetly opened a space for an interpretation attentive not to its *logical*, but to its *affective* movement. They have put us in a position to refuse the scholastic bias that only reads scholarly texts through the filter of the theory or social determinations behind them, so that we find ourselves now faced with a voice stripped to its bare argumentation. But what lesson can we draw from this frail vulnerability?

A recent work by Jacques Derrida exemplifies, I think, the tone to adopt in conclusion. *Chaque fois unique, la fin du monde* (*The Work of Mourning*) is a collection of texts written by the philosopher to pay homage to his deceased friends.[27] I will only retain the following trait, which marks an ethical preoccupation: in each case, Derrida explores the way in which these figures envisaged death, and the discovery of how each of them confronted that eventuality seems to him to be the most appropriate way of keeping their singular voice alive. The dead bequeath us, as it were, the always timely legacy of their relation to death. And to pay them homage is to be able to hear what they have left for us to hear.

Beneath its logical structure, the article devoted to Apollinaire perhaps bears witness, in its affective register, to the ethic that Bourdieu advocated when confronted with illness and death. The text begins with these words: ' "Autumn ill and adored", autumn adored *because* of its illness, because its mortality', and ends with these: 'Life is this continuous passage, right up to the ultimate discontinuity.' The ethical relation to literature makes possible, here, not the formulation of a researcher faced with objects he seeks to explain, as in the text on Ponge, but the expression of a personal relation to the 'flight of time', paradoxically muted by a mode of reading which signals that *pathos* here takes precedence over *logos*. The unusual tone of this article would then suggest that we, ourselves, should carry away the 'philosophical lesson (. . .) inscribed in autumn', that of a stoical *amor fati*. '*Amor amoris fati*', Bourdieu says: agree to love even that love of destiny against which you have so often rebelled. We might then see, in this detour via Apollinaire, something like a surrender of the sociologist to nature, which his sociology would not have allowed him to pronounce.

NOTES

1   Pierre Bourdieu, with Loïc Wacquant, *Réponses. Pour une anthropologie réflexive* (Paris: Seuil, 1992), 180.

2   Pierre Bourdieu, 'Apollinaire, Automne malade', *Cahiers d'Histoire des littératures romanes/Romanistische Zeitschrift für Literaturgeschichte* 3–4 (1995), 330–3. John Speller's English translation, 'Apollinaire, Autumn Ill', is included in the present special issue (see below, 131–6). Page references for this translation are followed by those for Bourdieu's original French text.

3   Yvette Delsault and Marie-Christine Rivière, *Bibliographie des travaux de Pierre Bourdieu, suivi d'un entretien sur l'esprit de la recherche* (Pantin: Le Temps des Cerises, 2002).

4   With the exception of Anna Boschetti, in *La Poésie est partout. Apollinaire, homme-époque* (Paris: Seuil, 2001), 185.

5   If we consider simply the domain of literature, the least used or least discussed articles by Bourdieu are notably: 'Nécessiter', in *Francis Ponge*, edited by Jean-Marie Gleize (Paris: Éditions de l'Herne, 1986), 434–7 and 'Le démontage impie de la fiction: l'esthétique negative de Stéphane Mallarmé', *Stanford Slavic Studies* 4:1 (1991), 145–50 (translation by Vinay Swamy, 'Mallarmé's Game of Poetry', *To be: 2B* 14 (1999), 32–5).

6   See, for example, Pierre Bourdieu, *Pascalian Meditations*, translated by Richard Nice (Stanford: Stanford University Press, 2000), 142–3: 'The agent engaged in practice knows the world but with a knowledge which (...) is not set up in the relation of externality of a knowing consciousness. (...) He feels at home in the world because the world is also in him, in the form of habitus, a virtue made of necessity which implies a form of love of necessity, *amor fati*.'

7   These considerations only push to their ultimate consequences Bourdieu's radical critique of the *scholastic fallacy*: (a) the logic of practice is not to be confused with the logic of theory; (b) theorizing is to be viewed as a practice inscribed in social universes; (c) this strictly social assignation of the diverse forms of theorizing is to be considered, in the last instance, as a specifically sociological form of epistocentrism. In other words, while the practical sense *of the sociologist* may have led him to theorize in a certain way, explaining this does not mean one must reproduce the same relation to theory: Bourdieu's own epistemology allows us to imagine that in his search for reflexively controlled logical coherence there were logics at work which could not be subsumed solely by the epistemology or sociology of scholarly activities.

8 Pierre Bourdieu, *The Rules of Art: Genesis and Structure of the Literary Field*, translated by Susan Emanuel (Cambridge: Polity Press, 1996).

9 See for example Pierre Bourdieu, 'Reading, readers, the literate, literature', in *In Other Words*, translated by Matthew Adamson (Stanford: Stanford University Press, 1990), 94–105, especially 95: 'One of the illusions of the *lector* is that which consists in forgetting one's own social conditions of production, and unconsciously universalizing the conditions of possibility of one's own reading. Inquiring into the conditions of this type of practice known as reading means inquiring into how *lectores* are produced, how they are selected, how they are educated, in what schools, etc. One would have to carry out a sociology of the success, in France, of structuralism, of semiology and of all the forms of reading, "symptomatic" or other. One would need to ask, for instance, whether semiology was not a way of producing an *aggiornamento* of the old tradition of "explication de textes" and of making it possible, at the same time, to redeploy a certain kind of literary capital.'

10 On the effects of canonization, which are regrettable according to Bourdieu, see the pages devoted to Baudelaire in *Pascalian Meditations*, 85–92.

11 I would like to take this opportunity to thank Anna Boschetti, Joseph Jurt and Henning Krauss, who have very kindly tried, unfortunately in vain, to help me to elucidate the circumstances under which the 1995 article was written and published.

12 Pierre Bourdieu, in Pierre Bourdieu and Loïc J. Wacquant, *An Invitation to Reflexive Sociology* (Cambridge: Polity Press, 1992), 207–8.

13 Pierre Bourdieu, *Homo Academicus*, translated by Peter Collier (Stanford: Stanford University Press, 1988), 149.

14 Pierre Bourdieu, *Masculine Domination*, translated by Richard Nice (Stanford: Stanford University Press, 2001), 81.

15 Pierre Bourdieu, *The Logic of Practice*, translated by Richard Nice (Stanford: Stanford University Press, 1990), 67.

16 Pierre Bourdieu, *Distinction*, translated by Richard Nice (Cambridge, MA: Harvard University Press), 77.

17 Jean-Claude Passeron, *Le Raisonnement sociologique. Un espace non poppérien de l'argumentation* (Paris: Albin Michel, 2006), 329–58.

18 See Pierre Bourdieu, *Distinction*, 258 (for Borges), 585, note 32 (for Perec), and 596, note 13 (on *The Trial*, which 'offers an exemplary image of this desperate striving to regain a social identity that is by definition ungraspable, being the infinite limit of all categoremes, all imputations'); or *Pascalian Meditations*, 24 (for Zola, whose evocation remains 'still derealized by literary stylization'), 198 (for La Rouchefoucauld), and 229 (on *The Trial* as a 'model of a social universe dominated by (...) an absolute and unpredictable power, capable of inducing extreme anxiety, by condemning its victim to very strong investment combined with very great insecurity').

19　And much more than Claudel or Gide, to whom Bourdieu regularly alludes, but as if in passing (see for example *The Logic of Practice*, 67; *Distinction*, 415; *Pascalian Meditations*, 69).

20　In a footnote of his own, Bourdieu writes: 'The text refers here to a Proustian text other than *La Recherche*: "Sentiments filiaux d'un parricide", in Marcel Proust, *Pastiches et mélanges* (Paris: Gallimard, 1970), 200.'

21　Pierre Bourdieu, *Distinction*, 21.

22　I develop this idea in my doctoral thesis, pointing out for example that the *literary* genesis of the petit-bourgeois has never been problematized as such by Marxist historians or sociologists, which suggests that its apparent obviousness may be a product of the 'invitations' of a still vigorous literary imagination as much as the rigorous demonstration of its empirical existence. See Jérôme David, *Éthiques de la description. Naissance de l'imagination typologique en France dans le roman et la sociologie (1820–1860)* (Université de Lausanne et Paris: EHESS, 2006).

23　Pierre Bourdieu, 'Nécessiter', 436–7.

24　Pierre Bourdieu in Bourdieu and Wacquant, *An Invitation to Reflexive Sociology*, 199. [Translator's note: the last sentence does not appear in this form in the English version of the book, and I have thus departed from the text for this.]

25　A passing reference to Cervantes in *Pascalian Meditations* ('letting time take its time', 228) may only have been meant, therefore, to save the phrase from its exclusive association with Mitterrandism, by attributing it to the altogether more famous and older author who coined it. And it seems that reading a work by E. L. Santner (*My Own Private Germany. Daniel Paul Schreiber's Secret History of Modernity* (Princeton: Princeton University Press, 1996)), in the interval between *Distinction* and *Pascalian Meditations*, made Bourdieu aware of new characteristics of *The Trial* by Kafka (see *Pascalian Meditations*, 72).

26　See for example Jacques Rancière, 'Le concept d'anachronisme et la vérité de l'historien', *L'Inactuel* 6 (1996), 53–68, and Georges Didi-Huberman, *Devant le temps. Histoire de l'art et anachronisme des images* (Paris: Minuit, 2000).

27　Jacques Derrida, *Chaque fois unique, la fin du monde* (Paris: Galilée, 2003). Originally published in English as Jacques Derrida, *The Work of Mourning*, edited by Pascale-Anne Brault and Michael Naas (Chicago: Chicago University Press, 2001).

Apollinaire, Autumn Ill

Pierre Bourdieu

AUTUMN ILL

> Autumn ill and adored
> You will die when the storm blows in the rose gardens
> When snow will have fallen
> In the orchards
>
> Poor autumn
> Die in whiteness and riches
> Of snow and ripe fruit
> While far up in the sky
> Sparrowhawks glide
> Over the foolish, dwarfish, greenhaired nymphs
> Who have never loved
>
> On the distant tree line
> The stags have belled
>
> And how I love — oh season — your murmurings
> The fruit falling with no one to gather it
> The wind and the forest weep
> All their tears in autumn leaf by leaf
> > The leaves
> > We trample
> > The train
> > Rolls by
> > Life
> > Flows away[1]

'Autumn ill and adored', autumn adored *because of* its illness, because of its mortality. Is not Apollinaire, the poet of the flux of time, of the

Paragraph 35.1 (2012): 131–136
DOI: 10.3366/para.2012.0046
© Edinburgh University Press
www.eupjournals.com/para

death of love, also the poet of the love of death, of the love of time passing, of the love of love as the terrain *par excellence* of this frailty?

The poet addresses autumn to announce its destiny, its final hour. He is the *vates*, the soothsayer, who says to autumn that it has had its moment, that its time has come or at least will come soon. There follows a series of antitheses: the wind and roses, the snow and the orchard, winter and spring, death and youth. From the future (you will die) Apollinaire shifts into the *future anterior* (when snow will have fallen), the future accomplished, that is the future already past, the tense of prophecy, which speaks of the future as if it had already happened.

The spring, the roses, the rose garden. Spring is the season of innocence, of hope and fragility. Autumn is the season of transition and decline, when the midday sun begins to set; the frailest of seasons, the most temporal of times. The wind is the west wind dear to Debussy, the wind that brings death to the rose gardens, a violent wind (underlined by the alliteration of 'r'). Petals that blow away, roses that lose their flowers, the poem is like a dramatized version of Ronsard's elegy. This image of violence is redoubled: the snow, a mortal whiteness, a cruel coldness, which burns and destroys silently, without a sound as it falls, comes to complete the brutal and sudden onslaught of the wind.

An Exhortation to Amor Fati

The poet pronounces the *fatum*, but also proffers an exhortation to *amor fati*. From the future anterior of prophesy, he jumps suddenly, at the beginning of the stanza, to the imperative. 'Die', accept death, learn how to die. He gives autumn a lesson in philosophy, which consists, simply, of drawing a lesson in philosophy that is already inscribed in autumn.

Die. Accept your destiny, which is to die. *Ama fatum*. But to accept one's destiny is, for autumn, to *die in beauty*, which is to say 'to die in whiteness and richness', two words which, by their alliance, remind us of the preceding stanza, which is to say the snow, a sumptuous shroud in the orchard, a menaced abundance. But the antithesis becomes a synthesis: the mortal snow and the richness of ripe fruits are reconciled in the *fatal beauty* of a luxurious decadence, so profoundly in harmony with the *fin-de-siècle* spirit. The beauty of autumn, like the beauty of Mélisande, is a mortal beauty, adorned with the strange and distant aura of those who are destined soon to die. Love your destiny, because it will be beautiful if you love it, if you love it for its beauty. Love of death, which makes death beautiful, decadent love of decadence, this is the very spleen of the *fin de siècle*.

The Fatal Moment

But in the clear, icy silence a sparrowhawk glides; a predatory bird that circles, and waits to swoop down from on high on its prey. A symbol of the present moment in suspension, of the menaced present and a menacing, imminent presence; a fatal instant, a dire moment of destiny and death. 'While far up in the sky/Sparrowhawks glide'. The theme of distance, charged with all kinds of menace (which will appear again, 'On the distant tree line'), with all kinds of anxiety: the distance is the locus of our fears, which are all the more menacing for being undefined. 'On the distant tree line/The stags have belled'. A song of love and death, a song that announces death, like the hunting horns that sing of death in the distance, and which haunt the œuvre of Debussy.

> The sound of a horn wails in the woods
> In seemingly orphaned affliction.[2]

The fatal moment has arrived: death bears down on the evil nymphs, green and sultry, deformed ('dwarfish') and sterile ('who have never loved').

Resignation

The poet declares himself: he speaks in the first person ('And how I love') and to declare his love to autumn (the culmination of the whole logical and affective movement of the poem). The poet loves autumn and what he loves in her is exactly what he has been describing, the slow astronomical and cosmic degenerescence, that of the twilight and old age, the melancholy drawn–out death of summer (which Debussy evokes in *Brouillards, Feuilles mortes, Soupirs,* or *Le son du cor s'afflige*). 'Autumn ill and adored': the poet loves autumn because of its illness. What he loves in autumn is the death of autumn, just as he loves in love the death of love; his love of love is a love of death.

The poet has reached that state of *amor fati* to which he had exhorted autumn. And at the same time the joy of time regained. He loves in autumn the love of destiny, the fruits of autumn fall without being collected, giving themselves up to death. To love autumn, the most seasonal of seasons ('oh season'), is to attain *amor amoris fati*, the ultimate form of *amor fati*. It is to love in the world all that is fleeting, fragile, elusive, the Heraclitean flux and the fluidity of time passing, of the days and the loves which fly by.

> The days pass and the weeks pass
> Neither time
> Nor loves return
> Beneath the Pont Mirabeau flows the Seine
>
> Autumn is dead, remember that.[3]

Or again:

> In the fog a bent-over peasant walks by
> With his ox slowly in the autumn fog.[4]

One thinks of the painting by Turner, in which one can hardly tell if the train is emerging from the fog or whether it is disappearing into it forever. Like Debussy and the impressionist painters, Apollinaire seems set on capturing the ungraspable, the most elusive, futile and humble details, *Pas sur la neige*, *Brouillards* or *Feuilles mortes*. And everywhere the river is present, the Seine which, like life, flows and flows:

> I was walking by the Seine,
> An old book under my arm
> The river is like my grief
> It flows and never dries up.[5]

'Everything passes', time, love, life, grief, but that is not the last word in this philosophy. Against the elegiac conception of duration, which sees in time the cause of all misery, mourning, not without complacency, the transitory and transient nature of all realities inscribed within time, Apollinaire, close to Schopenhauer in this respect (who was a very fashionable reference in the literary circles of the time), opposes a sort of optimistic, even joyful acquiescence to time and to the temporal destiny of man: a love of time in its essential ephemerality and of man as a transient being, who never ceases to pass, who does nothing but pass.

Apollinaire, in a sort of decrescendo combined with a diminuendo apt to express a vanishing into the distance, rediscovers a technique already employed to the same ends by Victor Hugo in 'Les Djinns':

> Everything flows
> Everything passes,
> Space
> Effaces
> The sound.

The music of poetry, like the elusive and fleeting life it evokes, vanishes progressively, in three-syllable lines, into the silence.

> The leaves
> We trample
> The train
> Rolls by
> Life
> Flows away

One thinks of all those pieces of music (*Fêtes*, *Sirènes* or *Nuages*[6]) in which what is called the perfect cadence, a sort of clear and distinct break between music and silence, life and death, gives way to a continuous progress towards silence, to a gradual fading of the elusive threshold where the transition from totality to nothingness takes place, where existence passes into non-existence. Life is this continuous passage, right up until the ultimate discontinuity.

Translated by John Speller

NOTES

1 Translator's note: This poem can be found in translation (as 'Sickly Autumn') in Guillaume Apollinaire, *Alcools*, translated by Anne Hyde Greet (Berkeley: University of California Press, 1965), 193. The verse translations in the present article are my own. The article was originally published as Pierre Bourdieu, 'Apollinaire, Automne malade', *Cahiers d'Histoire des littératures romanes/Romanistische Zeitschrift für Literaturgeschichte* 19:3–4 (1995), 330–3. It is reproduced by kind permission of the original publishers and Pierre Bourdieu's estate.

2 Translator's note: These lines are taken from the poem by Paul Verlaine, 'Le son du cor s'afflige vers les bois', from the collection *Sagesse* (1881), and set to music by Claude Debussy in 1891.
3 Translator's note: These lines are from, respectively, the poems 'Mirabeau Bridge' ('Le Pont Mirabeau') and 'The Farewell' ('L'Adieu') in Apollinaire, *Alcools*, 15, 89.
4 Translator's note: From the poem 'Autumn' ('Automne') in Apollinaire, *Alcools*, 129.
5 Translator's note: From the poem 'Marie' in Apollinaire, *Alcools*, 81.
6 Translator's note: These are the three compositions that make up Debussy's *Nocturnes* (1897–99).

Notes on Contributors

Jeremy Ahearne is Professor of French Studies at the University of Warwick. He is author of *Michel de Certeau: Interpretation and its Other* (1995), *Between Cultural Theory and Policy: The Cultural Policy Thinking of Pierre Bourdieu, Michel de Certeau and Régis Debray* (2004) and *Intellectuals, Culture and Public Policy in France: Approaches from the Left* (2010). He is editor and translator of *French Cultural Policy Debates: A Reader* (2002) and co-editor of *Intellectuals and Cultural Policy* (2007).

Anna Boschetti is former Professor of French Literature at the University of Venice. She is author of *Sartre et 'Les Temps modernes': une entreprise intellectuelle* (1985) (*The Intellectual Enterprise: Sartre and 'Les Temps Modernes'* (1988)); *La Poésie partout: Apollinaire, homme-époque (1898–1918)* (2001) and *La Rivoluzione simbolica di Pierre Bourdieu* (2003). She is editor of *L'Espace culturel transnational* (2010).

Jérôme David is Professor of French Literature at the University of Geneva. His fields of study include the comparative history of literature and social sciences and the global history of literature. He has published a book on the social history of 'novelistic types' in nineteenth-century French literature, entitled *Balzac, une éthique de la description* (2010). He is currently working on a history of the aesthetic category of 'world literature' (to be published by Les Prairies ordinaires, Paris).

Michel Hockx is Professor of Chinese at SOAS, University of London. He has done research on literary communities in early twentieth-century China and, more recently, on contemporary Chinese internet literature. His main Bourdieu-inspired publications are the edited volume *The Literary Field of Twentieth-Century China* (1999) and the monograph *Questions of Style: Literary Societies and Literary Journals in Republican China, 1911–1937* (2003).

Paragraph 35.1 (2012): 137–138
DOI: 10.3366/para.2012.0047
© Edinburgh University Press
www.eupjournals.com/para

Jeremy F. Lane is an Associate Professor in the Department of French and Francophone Studies at the University of Nottingham. He is the author of *Pierre Bourdieu: A Critical Introduction* (2000) and *Bourdieu's Politics: Problems and Possibilities* (2006). He is currently completing a book project on the reception of jazz in France between 1918 and 1945.

Gisèle Sapiro is Director of Research at the CNRS and Director of Studies at the École des Hautes Études en Sciences Sociales. She is also head of the Centre Européen de Sociologie et de Science Politique, Paris. Her interests include the sociology of intellectuals, literature and politics, publishing and translation, and the international circulation of cultural products and ideas. She is the author of *La Guerre des écrivains, 1940–1953* (1999; forthcoming in English translation with Duke University Press), and *La Responsabilité de l'écrivain. Littérature, droit et morale en France (XIXᵉ–XXIᵉ siècles)* (2011), and of numerous articles. She is also editor or co-editor of *Pour une histoire des sciences sociales* (2004), *Pierre Bourdieu, sociologue* (2004), *Translatio. Le marché de la traduction en France à l'heure de la mondialisation* (2008), *Les Contradictions de la globalisation éditoriale* (2009), and *L'Espace intellectuel en Europe* (2009).

John Speller teaches modern languages and the sociology of organizations at the International Faculty of Engineering, Łódź (Poland). He is author of the full-length study *Bourdieu and Literature* (2011).

EU Authorised Representative:

Easy Access System Europe Mustamäe tee 50, 10621 Tallinn, Estonia

gpsr.requests@easproject.com

Printed and bound by CPI Group (UK) Ltd, Croydon, CR0 4YY

09/06/2025

01897303-0002